D0927181

Gender, Doctrine, and God

GENDER, DOCTRINE, & GOD

The Shakers and Contemporary Theology

LINDA A. MERCADANTE

ABINGDON PRESS
Nashville

GENDER, DOCTRINE, AND GOD

Copyright © 1990 by Linda A. Mercadante

All rights reserved.
No part of this work may be reproduced or transmitted in any form or by any means, electronic or mechanical, including photocopying and recording, or by any information storage or retrieval system, except as may be expressly permitted by the 1976 Copyright Act or in writing from the publisher. Requests for permission should be addressed in writing to Abingdon Press, 201 Eighth Avenue South, Nashville, TN 37202.

This book is printed on acid-free paper.

Library of Congress Cataloging-in-Publication Data

Mercadante, Linda A., date.
  Gender, doctrine, and God : the Shakers and contemporary theology
  / Linda A. Mercadante
    p.   cm.
  Includes bibliographical references.
  ISBN 0-687-14041-2 (alk. paper)
    1. Femininity of God—History of doctrines. 2. God—Fatherhood—History of doctrines. 3. Shakers—Doctrines—History. 4. Shakers—Influence. 5. Theology, Doctrinal—United States—History—20th century. I. Title.
  BX9778.G7M47   1990
  231'.4—dc20   90-33347
                                                                      CIP

Grace Hauenstein Library
   Aquinas College
Grand Rapids, MI 49506

MANUFACTURED IN THE UNITED STATES OF AMERICA

For David,
who shared the first year and a half of his life
with the creation of this book

PREFACE AND ACKNOWLEDGMENTS

My introduction to Shaker life and theology began in the summer of 1981 during a vacation in New England. My husband, Charles Hamilton, and I were camping in New Hampshire when we saw signs pointing to the Shaker Village at Canterbury and decided to visit. Like many visitors before us, we were immediately impressed by the sense of harmony and peacefulness pervading the place. When a guide briefly mentioned the Shaker belief in a "Father-Mother" God, I realized I had encountered something worth investigating more deeply. I met with Eldress Bertha Lindsay afterward and asked for more information about the Shaker understanding of God. She said that theology was not her particular purview, but directed me to some helpful literature. I was struck by her enigmatically reticent and unhurriedly calm attitude, a quality I was to notice in the other Shakers I met in the course of doing research for this book.

Two different sets of people, places, and institutions were important in the creation of this book. The initial work was begun at Princeton Theological Seminary, in Princeton, New Jersey, a location just south of the northeastern branch of Shakerism. It was completed at the Methodist Theological School, Delaware, Ohio, which is located in the midst of the area that was the western branch of the Shaker Society.

At first the idea of studying the Shakers and their doctrine of God, especially as a potential resource for contemporary theology, was considered somewhat unusual by friends at Princeton Theological Seminary. But Dr. Karlfried Froehlich and Dr. Kathleen McVey gave the initial encouragement that I needed. My effort to focus on Shaker theology, however, was especially nurtured by Dr. Mark Kline Taylor, who, with his interest in religion as a cultural system as well as his grasp of contemporary feminist theology, immediately shared my excitement for the topic. During this work, Dr. Lois Gehr Livezey ensured that a spectrum of feminist theology and critique were carefully integrated into the entire project. Dr. John Wilson of Princeton University suggested ways the Shakers fit into the context of American religious history, and Dr. Robley Whitson served as an expert on Shaker sources. Dr. Mary Ford was a faithful and stimulating dialogue partner during the early research and writing stages of the book.

The receptive and supportive climate at the Methodist Theological School greatly facilitated the completion of this project. The encouragement and consideration of my colleagues and the enthusiasm of my students (as well as their willingness to hear yet one more example from Shakerism), have helped keep my interest in the topic alive. In addition, the opportunity I have had in the classroom to pursue relevant issues in the doctrine of God, the history of doctrine, and feminist theology has also done much to advance the focus, presuppositions, and conclusions of my study of the Shakers.

Thanks are due to the librarians and staff of the following institutions for their time and assistance: Hancock Shaker Village and Library, Pittsfield, Massachusetts; the Emma B. King Library and the Shaker Museum, Old Chatham, New

York; the Henry Francis DuPont Winterthur Museum, Winterthur, Delaware; the Fruitlands Museum, Harvard, Massachusetts; the Shaker Village at Canterbury, New Hampshire; Shaker Village of Pleasant Hill, Kentucky; and the Otterbein Home, Warren County, Ohio (formerly the Shaker's Union Village). In particular I would like to thank the Shakers, staff (especially Paige), and volunteers at the Sabbathday Lake, Maine, Shaker community who accommodated another researcher eager to explore their resources and ask questions. I am grateful for the opportunity to dine with them on various occasions, attend meeting, and for the chance to discuss Shakerism and Shaker theology with Brother Theodore Johnson.

The staff of the following institutions are also to be thanked for their assistance: Princeton Theological Seminary's Speer Library, especially Archivist William O. Harris, who uncovered a wealth of previously uncatalogued Shaker materials; Princeton University's Firestone Library; the Library of Congress Rare Book and Manuscript Divisions, Washington, D.C.; the Ohio Historical Society Library and Archives Division, Columbus, Ohio; and The Ohio State University's William Oxley Thompson Memorial Library, Columbus, Ohio (especially R. A. Tibbetts). Special thanks must be given to the staff of Methodist Theological School's John W. Dickhaut Library. These gracious co-workers were always willing to order "just a few more things" for me.

Several meetings of the American Academy of Religion, as well as of the regional Mid-Atlantic and Midwest American Academy of Religion, enabled me to present parts of this book in various sessions. Participants at the 1987 National Council of Churches conference on Language, Thought and Social Justice, Stony Point, New York, also offered helpful perspectives on the research. The Columbus, Ohio, Cluster Faculty Women's Group read and critiqued an early draft of a portion of the book.

For help in completing this work, I would especially like to thank Dr. Davis Perkins, who appreciated the relevancy of the Shaker example for contemporary theology. His able assistance has been carried on by my present editor at Abingdon Press, Ulrike Guthrie. Not only did they aid the project, but both of them were especially considerate when our new son, David, arrived sooner than expected, and the proposed writing schedule had to be adjusted. I am especially grateful to friends and colleagues who read parts or all of the manuscript. Their excellent comments helped me to further clarify, organize, and state my main premises and conclusions. Thanks to Dorianne Perrucci, who gave up a very fine summer weekend to labor over the first draft (and to our friend Ginny Potter, who watched David while we worked); and also to able readers Dr. Elaine Ramshaw and Bertie Dell (both of whom labored over a Thanksgiving break to read the whole manuscript). And thanks to Dr. Joanmarie Smith, Dr. David Carr, Dr. William Soll, Dr. Dennis Prindle, and to Sherron Courneen, who read various chapters and offered excellent critiques. My husband, Chuck, always my "best editor," also gave up his Thanksgiving break to carefully critique the entire manuscript. In this and in his reading of earlier drafts, he was again successful at being "constructively critical."

Finally, essential ongoing support has come from my family and friends who provided the emotional ballast necessary to cope not only with a book, but with a baby and a new job—an exhilarating but at times overwhelming combination. Without the constant day-to-day efforts of my husband, Chuck, the support and baby-sitting assistance of my parents, Gene and Gerry Mercadante (when David and I stayed with them in New Jersey), and the reassuring expertise of "Grandma" Moore and Diane McGraw, this book would never have gotten written.

L.A.M.
Delaware, Ohio
December 1989

CONTENTS

INTRODUCTION

As long as we have all male Gods in the heavens we shall have all male rulers on the earth. But when the heavenly Mother is revealed, and is sought unto as freely and confidingly as the Heavenly Father, then will woman find her proper sphere of action.

Antoinette Doolittle, *The Shaker* II
(June 1872)

From the beginning of their history, the Shakers have inspired strong emotional reactions, ranging from romantic reverie to spontaneous loathing. For some, this experiment in communal, celibate, and ordered living—where impassioned worship balanced strict social order—has sparked a vision of peace and harmony, gender equality, and mutual cooperation. Yet for others the Shaker example has aroused fears of mass manipulation and control. That the group was founded by a woman, that it for a time elevated her to almost messianic proportions, and that it evolved an image of God as Father and Mother, has added to the intensity of the emotions inspired.

Today the movement to reconsider and expand gender imagery for God is also stirring a wide range of emotions. On one hand, some link an almost millennialist vision of peace, equality, and mutual cooperation to the proposed uncoupling from exclusively male God imagery. At the very least, the inclusion of female imagery for God is seen as necessary for the viability of the Christian faith in the modern world. Much hope rests, therefore, in ongoing efforts to expand imagery for God in liturgy, language, and theology.

On the other hand, some people in the church are gripped by an almost apocalyptic fear, convinced that introducing female images for God would be tantamount to forsaking the Christian faith. At the least, many believe such changes in the religion's core symbolism are unnecessary and distracting. And significant numbers refuse even to discuss the matter, so strong are the feelings and so confused are the issues. The contemporary church is seriously divided, even paralyzed, over the subject of gender imagery for God.

Although those on the opposite ends of the spectrum agree that changes in God imagery would be revolutionary, the contemporary church as a whole cannot reach consensus about whether such changes are desirable or even possible. My own conviction, when I began the research for this book, was that the development of gender-inclusive imagery for God was a necessary and essential task for the church. I expected that this development would have major, beneficial impact on both women's and men's self-image, religious experience and church life, and possibly on societal structures as well.

But the task appeared so arduous and the resistance so deep-seated that it seemed advisable to step back and reflect on our theological options and practical methods in light of possible historical precedents. Thus I was attracted to the Shakers, since they were one of very few groups in Western Christianity that consistently focused on gender issues and used gender-inclusive imagery for God. It was encouraging to me that for much of their two-hundred-year history the Shakers understood God as encompassing both male and female, worked out this belief theologically, celebrated it in liturgy, and lived it in social structure. Their success in cultivating the image of God as Father and Mother suggested to me that widespread use of inclusive imagery for God was realizable. Their gender-parallel social structure, attention to the religious experience of both women and men, stress on cooperation rather than competition, and communal orientation added weight to the contemporary argument that gender-inclusive imagery for God has profound, important, and desirable effects.

I hoped that the study of the Shakers would provide some data about the extent to which change can be provoked by expanding our imagery for God, the shape that such changes might take, and the social realities necessary to facilitate such changes. Equally important—especially given the theological and liturgical impasse in the contemporary church over the gender-imagery issue—I expected that close attention to the Shaker doctrine of God would produce insights that could aid the contemporary theological discussion. Perhaps certain key elements of their understanding of God could transcend their context and prove useful to the contemporary constructive theological work on gender and God. Approaching the Shakers from this perspective has led to unexpected results.

Close attention to the Shaker example has revealed that they neither conform to nor confirm some of our modern theories about gender-inclusive imagery for God. Several elements of the Shaker story strike discordant notes and deserve serious reflection. Three are especially prominent. First, historical evidence shows that Shaker gender-inclusive imagery for God did not come at the beginning of their history or function as keynote. Rather than gender-inclusive God imagery producing personal and structural change, such changes produced the imagery. The development of the Shaker doctrine of God followed the institution of their gender-parallel work and social structures, as well as the formation of their group self-consciousness.

Second, their famed gender equality, upon careful inspection, reveals serious flaws on both the theological and practical levels. Although other scholars have intimated this, the point bears further elaboration. For this factor suggests that we may need to modify or refine the modern assumption that there is a positive correlation between gender-inclusive God imagery and egalitarian social structure. At the very least, the Shaker example highlights some theological hazards in the current work with gender imagery for God.

And, finally, a study of Shaker materials suggests that Shaker believers' actual use of female imagery for God in their personal expressions of faith was uneven and sporadic. Indeed, this appears to have been the case even during a pivotal phase in their history when conditions were ripe for the widespread use of female imagery. In spite of a climate conducive to the use of female God images, many believers' religious experience does not seem to have been deeply affected by these images. This aspect of Shakerism has gone largely unnoticed in Shaker studies. Yet it is this factor that may pose the most serious challenge to the contemporary discussion about inclusive imagery, requiring a reconsideration of current theories about gender imagery for God.

This book, therefore, has gone through a long metamorphosis during which its premises and conclusions have changed significantly. The work began as a quest to find theological clues and encouragement in a historical group that—like many in and out of the church today—repudiated exclusively male imagery for God. But the process of reflecting upon current theories about gender imagery in light of the evidence from the Shakers has made the work something different. What began as a search for clues to aid the current effort to introduce gender-inclusive imagery for God, and to support current theories about the influence of that imagery, became instead a reflection on the relationship between experience, imagery, and doctrine in the issue of gender and God.

The five chapters of this book will examine both the modern rationales for the use of gender-inclusive imagery for God, and the Shaker evidence that bears upon the relevant current issues. Chapter 1 will analyze some contemporary assumptions about the priority and power of gender-inclusive imagery for God, since the feminist critique makes essential claims about this. In the process, it will survey some major arguments for gender-inclusive God imagery, briefly highlighting the complex relationship between imagery, doctrine, and experience.

Chapter 2 will examine Shaker history and social structure in light of their development of a gender-inclusive doctrine of God. This is necessary since the Shaker story poses challenges to some current assumptions about the priority order in the doctrine/experience dynamic. This chapter will consider the formation of the Shaker doctrine of God in relationship to the formation of their gender-parallel social structure, the roles of women and men, the significance of the revival period, and relevant aspects of their numerical decline.

Chapter 3 will examine the Shaker doctrine of God, its images and theological insights, and the symbolic role of gender as reflected in several formative theological publications. The analysis will focus on the most comprehensive and authoritative presentations of these positions in the published works of Shaker theology. A close examination is necessary for two reasons. First, the fact that the Shakers' doctrine of God is gender-inclusive suggests that Shaker theology, however poorly realized in practice, presents a model of gender equality. Close analysis will allow this impression to be questioned. Second, such an examination also is critical because the Shakers explored various options in gender-inclusive imagery for God that still are viable possibilities for contemporary theology today.

Chapter 4 will examine Shaker testimonies of faith in order to understand the impact of the Society's gender-inclusive doctrine of God on average Shakers. This next step is critical in light of an important assumption in contemporary theology—and in the feminist work with gender-inclusive imagery—that religion as a cultural system has a profound experience-producing effect on adherents. It is not enough to simply analyze Shaker theology and social structure. To go beyond this and examine Shaker testimonies of faith can suggest—within the constraints of historical reconstruction—how committed Shakers internalized the counter-cultural view of a gender-inclusive God, and how influential this view was on their experience and expression of faith. Finally, chapter 5 will offer conclusions from the Shaker study, and examine the implications of these for the contemporary discussion.

CHAPTER ONE

GENDER IMAGERY FOR GOD: THE COMPLEXITY OF THE ISSUE

In the beginning, there was no discontent with God the Father. That is, the first women's rights activists in this century did not start out with a critique of God symbolism. Rather, women began with a critique of their own restricted conditions and cultural devaluation. The critique of the male image of God in Christianity has emerged from the struggle for the image of women. Once the image of women began to improve, a concern arose for the image of God.

Contemporary feminists are not the first to oppose the gender hierarchy in Christianity. Nearly two hundred years ago, a small communitarian group, the United Society of Believers in Christ's Second Appearing, or Shakers, expressed similar concerns. Although in many ways they differ from the contemporary movement, an examination of the Shakers offers valuable insights. For they not only questioned gender hierarchy, but also, in seeking to address this, they employed both gender-inclusive imagery for God and a gender-parallel social structure. The Shakers provide an illuminating set of data that may shed some light upon the current focus on imagery for God.

For today the image of God has become a focal symbol in the effort to achieve equal dignity and opportunity for women.[1] While there is a large segment of modern American feminism that is thoroughly secular, concerned primarily with legal and economic justice, there is also a

19

large and still growing component that is concerned with religious issues. Among this latter group, the image of God has become a rallying point. There is widespread agreement that our view of ourselves, society, and reality itself is intimately linked with our view of God. Our sacred symbols, especially our dominant images and metaphors for God, are inextricably linked with our self-image and our behavior. This consensus holds no matter how God is conceived: whether as the ultimate, the source of all, the ground of being, the transcendent power greater than ourselves, or the energy within. And this accord persists along with a recognition that words can never encompass God since they are at best analogical and inadequate.

In the last twenty years, numerous writers have argued persuasively that exclusively male imagery for God has had deleterious effects on Western religion and society. It is contended that such imagery has limited our knowledge of God and promoted the idolatrous worship of the male; further, some insist this male imagery has also been used to justify atrocities against women and that the sexism it supports is the primal form of human oppression.[2] The critique also has raised questions about the distinction between sexuality and gender. That is, the fact of two genders does not prove that there are ontological masculine and feminine principles. After several decades of protest, this critique of gender hierarchy—and its links with God imagery—has reached a considerable audience. There is a growing consensus that exclusively male imagery for God is inadequate.

Many feminists agree that the next step, and perhaps an even more difficult one, is to move beyond critique to construction: to convince people of the need to expand language and imagery for God beyond the exclusively male, and to reach consensus on the most adequate ways in which to do that. Those at work on this goal have offered a variety of rationales to explain why new imagery is needed. But the overall argumentation is complex, and different writers approach the issue from varying perspectives.

At least four major arguments or rationales exist in the contemporary discussion promoting gender-inclusive imagery for God, and many writers combine several of these approaches. It is important to gain clarity about these ways of arguing for expanding imagery for God. Without such clarity, efforts to address the problem run the risk of being diffused and uncoordinated.

Rationales for Expanding God Imagery

The Pragmatic Argument

The first argument will be termed pragmatic, since it is primarily concerned with results. Few feminist arguments proceed without at least a modified version of this approach. This argument does not prevent the making of truth-claims about God, but that is not the focus here. Rather, the emphasis is upon effecting change. According to this approach, expanding God imagery will have a beneficial effect on personal self-consciousness and societal structures. This widely used argument places a priority on the changing of symbols. It is true that many writers are careful not to make a simplistic one-way equation between symbol change and behavioral change. Nevertheless, there is a pervasive and definite assertion that, as Sallie McFague says, "a new imaginative picture of the relationship between God and the world must *precede* action" [emphasis mine].[3] Thus, in arguments for gender-inclusive God imagery that rely heavily on a pragmatic emphasis, the changing of religious symbols is held to have priority.

Language and imagery thus are understood to have a profound experience-shaping, even controlling, power. One writer puts it quite clearly: "Language can condition value structures and basic assumptions. It can control our beliefs about reality, our ways of thinking, and even how we think about thinking.[4] Given the intimate connection between values, thought, and behavior, many feminists stress changing language and imagery in order to facilitate the desired changes in relationships and societal institutions.

It is argued that changing the imagery for God will help alleviate women's sense of sacral unworthiness—that is, the feeling of devaluation that permeates women's self-consciousness as a result of constantly hearing the divine identified with maleness.[5] As Naomi Goldenberg says, using female imagery for God is expected to help transform into a sense of self-worth, affirmation, and identification with deity this "psychic oppression . . . [that] dup[es] women into believing that they are innately inferior to men."[6] Concomitantly, men are expected to become unburdened of their assumed responsibility to solely represent God and, in addition, to no longer deny in themselves all the attributes considered feminine.

It is still debated whether or not the human characteristics traditionally considered masculine and feminine are really properties of male and female, but few doubt that the cluster of attributes associated with males have been overvalued and those associated with females undervalued. The benefit of introducing female imagery and feminine characteristics into the God concept is expected to extend to the area of human relationships as well. As Joan Chamberlain Engelsman suggests:

> The recognition and elaboration of a feminine image of God should affect the image of real women . . . act[ing] as an antidote to the notions of masculine preeminence. Furthermore, it could give women a sense of dignity previously unknown. . . . In addition, an image of God with both masculine and feminine dimensions would dramatize the

*intra*sexual harmony of the divine which human beings could emulate in their own *inter*personal relationships.[7]

Beyond the transformation of personal self-consciousness and interpersonal relationships, the inclusion of female imagery for God is expected to help change society at large. There can be a somewhat millennialist quality to the literature that envisions the positive consequences for society that would be facilitated by a change in God imagery. Some have argued that if we locate in the divine those attributes commonly associated with women—life-affirming qualities such as birth-giving, nurture, support, relatedness, tenderness, and peace-making—we may have a chance not only of renewing humankind, but also of saving the earth from destruction.[8] Others have argued that the hierarchical patterns of the past must be eradicated, and that gender-inclusive imagery for God can play an important part in the process. According to Rosemary Ruether, the knowledge of communal personhood is the secret power of feminism, and its aim is

> the total abolition of the social pattern of domination and subjugation and the erection of a new communal social ethic. We need to build a new cooperative social order out beyond the principles of hierarchy, rule, and competitiveness. . . . We must create a living pattern of mutuality between men and women, between parents and children, among people in their social, economic, and political relationships and, finally, between mankind and the organic harmonies of nature.[9]

This stress on mutuality as opposed to hierarchy in human relationships is a hallmark of feminist theology and a significant part of the discussion about imagery for God.[10] In addition, ever since the second wave of feminism—beginning with the women's rights movement that emerged in the second half of the twentieth century—there has been an implicit assumption that movement toward gender equality would include the freedom for both women and men to choose whatever kind of work was fulfilling and socially useful. It has become largely accepted that to structure the division of labor along gender lines limits the abilities and development of both women and men.[11] Although this assumption is not always specifically mentioned, especially in theological discussions, it is an implicit part of the effort to change social, economic, and political relationships. As such, it is one more positive effect that gender-inclusive imagery for God is expected to facilitate.

The Neo-Pragmatic Argument

Sometimes, the pragmatic argument becomes combined with a focus on the needs and values of a particular situation to produce a second, different rationale. Here, the pragmatic emphasis on results, and the focus on context, come to dominate the discussion about God imagery in such a way that the making of truth-claims about God through imagery is considered illegitimate. This neo-pragmatic approach insists that when we speak of God, we do not describe an ontological reference point. Instead we create imagery for God that suits the goals and needs of a particular context. It is assumed that this imagery then will exercise its influence upon the culture.

There is a heuristic variation to this rationale that, although similar in argumentation to a full neo-pragmatic approach, makes an important distinction. This heuristic variation allows for the reality of God, although it considers truth-claims about God to be beyond the realm of the gender-imagery argument. While it is contended that the imaginative construal of imagery need not be fully relativistic, such that one image is as good as another, nevertheless theological construction is held to be, as Sallie McFague says, *"mostly* fiction." This implies that when circumstances change, so must the imagery. When evaluating images and metaphors for God, then, "the question we must ask is not whether one is true and the other false, but which one is a better portrait of Christian faith *for our day*."[12]

In a full neo-pragmatic approach, "constructing the concept of God"[13] in this way can become so situation-specific as to obviate all reference beyond the particular context. Thus this argument can move the imagery discussion toward a thorough uncoupling from theism altogether.[14] In the neo-pragmatic view, as presented for example by Sheila Greene Davaney, the contention is that "religious symbols are not interpreted as referential . . . of an assumed ontological reality. Instead they are recognized as human constructions that function to focus the world-view of which they are a part. . . . our Gods and Goddesses are the articulation of our values and hopes, not the foundation of certitude nor the promise of victory."[15]

In the neo-pragmatic argument, then, gender-inclusive imagery for God is simply the most adequate expression of contemporary values and goals today, and a necessary aid in achieving those goals. It makes no claims about the future, about experience of any reality beyond this worldly realm, or any truth-claims about a God who could be the source or reference point of this imagery.

The Apologetic Argument

A third argument for gender-inclusive imagery for God will be termed the apologetic, since it seeks to make God imagery persuasive, attractive, and relevant to today's situation. Like the neo-pragmatic argument, this approach focuses on the importance of understanding and meeting the needs of the contemporary context, arguing that gender-inclusive imagery for God better corresponds to the needs, values, and experience of modern people. But this argument does not obviate the making of truth-claims, although that is generally not the primary focus. Rather, the emphasis here is upon sensitivity to the human situation.

Although this argument can accompany the pragmatic approach, it in fact addresses the issue of gender imagery from an entirely different perspective. Indeed, in some ways these two arguments are incompatible. For instead of pointing to the experience-shaping power of God imagery, this approach insists that God imagery is dependent upon the context and experience of the believer. It is argued that imagery primarily is, or should be, expressive of experience and sensitive to context. When a God image no longer fulfills that function, it is dead and must be discarded.

This approach to sacred symbols is part of a liberal theology that takes the relevancy of the religion with utmost seriousness and gives it a central place. This theology assumes that behind religious imagery there is some universal spiritual experience that is accessible to a wide range of persons. When this theme is pursued fully, it becomes the fourth argument (discussed below), the argument from experience. But often in feminist literature the apologetic approach is focused primarily upon the material or world context, rather than upon the religious experience and the desire to express it in communicable categories.

The apologetic ability of a religion is seen as critical; for if a religion claims, as Christianity does, to be relevant and applicable regardless of era or culture, then that religion's primary symbols must be accessible to the people it seeks to address. This includes recognizing those people's ideals and values. Our society is beginning to recognize the full humanity of women, and the necessity for women to develop their abilities and use their resources for the betterment of self and society. Given our emerging cultural values and women's experience of growing freedom, a religion that insists that ultimate reality is better depicted by solely masculine imagery soon will come to lose its persuasiveness. As Elizabeth A. Johnson writes, the adequacy of an idea of God is tested by its ability "to integrate the complexity of present experience into itself. If the idea of God does not keep pace with developing reality, the power of experience pulls people on and the god dies."[16]

Although some Christians may make a virtue of the "Christ against culture" paradigm,[17] those who intend to address their message to a particular culture must be relevant to it. Some modern writers, however, aspire to more than mere relevancy and suggest that when the Christian faith is made more apologetically attractive through changing its imagery for God, there may be an additional benefit, that is, a spiritual revival within Christianity. Engelsman, for example, suggests that "when the *ikon* of God as father is replaced by a multiplicity of images, including the feminine, Christianity may undergo a rebirth which might expand, rather than diminish, its appeal."[18]

The Argument from Experience

The argument furthest away from the reasoning of the pragmatic argument is what will be termed the argument from experience. Few writers who argue for gender-inclusive God imagery take a fully neo-pragmatic stance, or restrict themselves to the self-limiting scope of the pragmatic and apologetic arguments. Except for those who hold resolutely to the neo-pragmatic argument, the force of the gender-imagery argument leads many to make truth-claims, even if only implicitly.

The argument from experience, in the discussion to expand God imagery, goes beyond simple pragmatics or context-focused apologetics. Here the focus is on experience, but not as an end in itself. Thus, while experience is recognized to be inevitably contextual, it also is understood to give valid information about—or to be a true expression of—ontological reality and God. Experience can be seen to verify and correct theological imagery and concepts. Or theological imagery can be understood primarily as the expression of a valid religious experience. In both cases, experience is the source of theological reflection. The resulting truth-claims can refer either to God directly, or to some ultimate value that serves as the ground of being.

Like some versions of the apologetic method, this argument takes a significantly different approach from the pragmatic and neo-pragmatic. Truth claims can be subtle or quite explicit. In either case, the key is that images and metaphors are meant primarily not to control or shape experience, but rather to express experience. Religious images thus principally express transcendent personal experience with the divine, the ultimate, or the primal source of all being. That imagery is valid, then, that expresses religious experience.

For instance, Rosemary Ruether locates this reference point of truth as "God/ess," a term that serves "to point toward that yet unnameable understanding of the divine that would transcend patriarchal limitations and signal redemptive experience for women as well as men."[19] For Carol Christ, this ultimate value and reference point is "women's creative powers and . . . human interdependence and connection with what patriarchal splitting has called 'the natural world' (as if there were any other). I believe that the symbol of Goddess has a particular power to evoke this."[20]

When the argument from experience is used to test the theological and conceptual adequacy of God imagery, it is argued that we can speak more clearly about God if gender-inclusive imagery is used. Since Christian tradition teaches that both men and women are made in God's image, inclusive imagery is an improved way of showing that God encompasses all of humankind. The clue[21] about God that we derive from the "imago dei" allows us to speak about God with some small measure of confidence.

But gender-inclusive imagery also reminds us that our language for God is merely analogical and thus inadequate and imprecise. This sort of "via negativa" points to the ultimate futility of trying to encompass God with human categories. Recognizing the incomprehensibility of God is much easier to achieve when we realize not only that God is not masculine, but also that God is not feminine.[22] Therefore, the smashing of the idolatry of exclusively male imagery can best be achieved by the concomitant inadequacy of calling God somehow female. A move to incorporate female images in our discussion of God will help unbind our view of God, free our imagination, and remind us that God cannot be controlled.

In the argument from experience, the mere changing of theological concepts is not considered an adequate way to affect experience. Imagery is seen primarily not to shape experience, but to facilitate the expression of experience. Yet the imagery changes that arise from experience are understood to have some influence as they further free the imagination to experience and express a relationship to ultimate reality. Thus, in the relationship between experience and theological idea, it is the religious imagination that serves as the fulcrum.

Experience can be translated into new images and concepts only when the religious imagination is allowed to operate freely. Sandra Schneiders explains that "our God image . . . is a function of the imagination," and for many people the problem is not first theological, but imaginative. There is today "a paralysis of the religious imagination" such that God simply cannot be imagined as feminine. Rethinking theological concepts alone is inadequate to cause the deep changes needed to heal the religious imagination. We need

> not only to think differently about God but to experience God differently. The imagination is accessible not primarily to abstract ideas but to language, images, interpersonal experience, symbolism, art—all the integrated approaches which appeal simultaneously to intellect, will, and feeling.[23]

Although changing imagery and language can help free the imagination and result ultimately in the formation of new theological ideas, a crucial goal is to facilitate religious experience and its expression.

From this perspective, female or gender-inclusive God imagery is trustworthy and valid because it articulates an authentic experience of the liberating God. When experience is claimed as the source and norm of expanded God imagery, the discussion often turns to the theme of liberation. From this perspective, God (or God/ess) is to be met wherever people struggle against oppression. For women contending against the oppression of masculinism, the Divine Liberator can be experienced in the midst of the struggle, among other women, and as a power that women can access. This encounter liberates us from the false dualism of nature and spirit, a primary component of patriarchal theology.

> The liberating encounter with God/ess is always an encounter with our authentic selves resurrected from underneath the alienated self. It is not experienced against, but in and through relationships, healing our broken relations with our bodies, with other people, with nature.[24]

This revelational experience of the divine is better expressed using female or gender-inclusive imagery. For in the midst of struggle God becomes known as the one who frees women. The experience reveals, and then repeatedly confirms, that this is the God who loves women and identifies with them.[25] It follows that female imagery for God should arise in particular from women, and have its greatest appeal to women.

The Interaction Between Experience, Imagery, and Doctrine

These very different approaches are included in the overall argumentation for gender-inclusive imagery for God. The discussion generally focuses on religious language and symbols, but it does not exclude the issue of doctrine. Imagery and doctrine are intimately linked. Doctrines, in essence, are communal norms. They organize and regularize the beliefs of a given group, are considered essential to the group's identity, and identify the faithful. Religious images and metaphors provide the more experientially linked component in doctrine.

Rather than being purely abstract intellectual conventions, doctrines blend both the conceptual and the imagistic sides of religious expression. Doctrine thus is connected to experience on both ends, in that it contains articulated, communally accepted experience, and it influences the interpretation of experience. Although there is an antithetical feeling in our individualistic age toward the constraints of communal norms, at base the discussion about gender imagery accepts the necessity of such standards. For in actuality the discussion of God imagery is a demand for the revitalization and improvement of communal norms. The debate over God imagery is a recognition that the doctrine of God should be connected to the experience of God.

Most theorists agree that even as doctrine and image help bring experience to articulation, they also help to shape experience. However, the various arguments for gender-inclusive imagery stress different sides of this dynamic. The pragmatic argument is primarily concerned with the shaping power of religious symbols and theological concepts. Although it does not focus on possible truth claims made by symbols, neither does it obviate them. The neo-pragmatic argument is, like the pragmatic, concerned with the shaping power of religious symbols, but does not admit the possibility of truth claims behind these symbols. The apologetic argument either can combine attention to context along with an expressive understanding of imagery, or it can stress only one of these two elements. Although, like the pragmatic argument, it does not deal primarily with truth claims, it does not prevent them. The experiential argument primarily focuses on the expressive character of imagery. It is different from the other approaches in that it can either implicitly or explicitly argue from a basis in the truth claiming power of imagery that arises from religious experience. These various rationales all are part of the effort to promote gender-inclusive imagery for God, but it must be asked whether they can co-exist without mutual contradiction.

If one accepts George Lindbeck's schematization of the nature of doctrine,[26] one may find these arguments not only are different, but also are in opposition. According to Lindbeck's schema, one perspective (the cultural-linguistic) understands doctrine to have a major shaping force in human experience. A second major perspective, the experiential-expressive, understands doctrine to essentially express experience. Although Lindbeck does not deal extensively with the problem of gender imagery, this schematization raises some questions about the inner consistency of the argumentation for gender-inclusive imagery. For while Lindbeck agrees that the process is a dynamic, rather than a one-way interaction, he insists that one side of the experience/doctrine interaction must become the leading partner.[27] In other words, either doctrine or experience must be seen to take the lead and have primary force in the dynamic.

Feminists seem to agree that one side of the dynamic must precede. Indeed, quite different strategies arise out of the different arguments for gender-inclusive God imagery. In the context of the gender imagery issue it makes a significant difference which side is stressed, for that choice determines the focus of attention and action. If doctrine and image are understood to exert a profound shaping, even controlling, influence over experience, doctrine and image will have a pivotal function. To effect change, one will begin with the language and imagery in liturgy, theology, and everyday conversation. Changes made there are then expected to filter down, affecting experience and behavior. And, in recognition of the transformative power of doctrine, one will have to be especially careful to develop consistent, consensual standards for imagery change. Changes in imagery and doctrine will be the main focus of action or have priority in addressing the problems attributed to the traditional mono-gendered understanding of God.

If, on the other hand, doctrine and imagery are considered primarily to reflect and express experience, attention needs to be focused on religious experience. Discrepancies between experience and doctrine will be judged as a failure of existing imagery to fully express current religious experience. Those who are attentive to this perspective must concentrate on encouraging, understanding, and expressing the experience itself, rather than starting at the other end by changing the images and language. An openness to varying expressions of experience and to a multiplicity of experiences is consistent with this view. But one cannot predict or control the imagery that emerges from this approach.

Approaches to Expanding God Imagery

The divergence in arguments for gender-inclusive imagery is repeated in varying methods available for expanding God imagery. There is no agreement on exactly *how* to expand our images and metaphors for God. Therefore, various approaches can and have been taken. First, it is possible to avoid the gender problem altogether. God can be referred to in non-personal terms, such as Power, Energy, Source, or Be-ing. This approach can highlight God's pervasive immanental presence yet divine difference from humans. However, many object that the traditional sense of personal relationship with the divine is lost. In addition, as McFague insists, personal terms represent important values that we must not abandon. "The qualities of personal relationship are needed in our time. . . . The problem . . . is not *that* personal metaphors and concepts have been used for God . . . [but] in the particular metaphors and concepts chosen" (emphasis mine).[28]

Another possibility is to retain the traditionally personal quality of God language, but eliminate its gender specificity. God can be referred to as Creator, Sustainer, Redeemer, or simply God. This can appeal to congregations sensitive to the feminist critique, for it allows some traditional understandings of God's action to be used while avoiding the complications of gender. However, since the experience of actual human relationship inevitably carries the element of gender, this approach makes it difficult to express religious experience in familiar, readily communicative ways. In addition, the image of God then conveys either a monodimensionality or a functionalism that does not well convey relationality.

It also is possible to use exclusively female imagery for God. This avoidance of male imagery altogether is done partly to prevent the perpetuation of the idolatrous elevation of the male. Some also believe that female imagery better expresses the nature of the divine. Female imagery can be parental (Mother), can focus on traditionally female values (sensuality, relationship)[29] and draw imagery from these attributes, or can replace the concept God with the concept Goddess. This approach has transforming potential, especially for women, since it radically breaks the idolatry of male imagery. Goddess symbolism affirms the legitimacy and beneficence of female power; it values the female body and the life cycle expressed in it; it makes a place for the use of women's will. Finally, it reaffirms women's bonds and heritage.[30] But many in the church balk at using Goddess symbolism. For some it is too radical a change, and for others it simply seems to replace one hegemony with another.

Another approach is the one the Shakers used of including both genders when referring to God. In this method, metaphors are derived from both male and female experience, as well as from the images and implications that Scripture and tradition provide.[31] The clear advantage is that this method retains both the traditionally personal quality of God language, and the belief that both male and female image God.

The image of God as Mother seems a logical starting place for female imagery. Commentators such as Sallie McFague contend that female imagery for God should include the maternal aspect, in spite of the risk of stereotyping, because "the symbolic material from the birthing and feeding process is very rich and for the most part has been neglected in establishment Christianity." The model of God as Mother, McFague adds, is especially powerful in "expressing the interrelatedness of all life."[32] Finally, gender-inclusive imagery can also move beyond understanding God as parental, that is, Father and Mother, and draw from other gendered human relationships, such as sister or gender-specific friend.

The difficulty comes in deciding the most theologically appropriate way to make God imagery gender-inclusive. At least three approaches to gender-inclusive imagery exist.[33] They will be discussed in more detail in chapter 5, but they can be briefly noted here. First, female-associated traits can be assigned to a God still imaged as essentially masculine. Second, God can be presented as consisting of masculine and feminine elements. Although the few instances of this in Christian theology have traditionally been done in a trinitarian form (usually by positing the Holy Spirit as the feminine element),[34] a non-trinitarian (often dual, or 'binitarian') variation also exists. Third, God can be understood as primarily a non-gendered spirit who is essentially one, yet who encompasses what we understand as male and female characteristics, and has an indivisible yet pluralistic quality that allows many different images and interactions to be used metaphorically. Since the Shakers wrestled with some of these same options in gender-inclusive imagery, a study of their theology and imagery presents a prime opportunity to explore the gender-inclusive approach.

Why Study the Shakers?

There are a number of compelling reasons for studying the Shakers. On the most foundational level, the Shakers are a marginalized tradition from our recent past (late eighteenth century to the present) whose theological insights and experiences have not been attended to with sufficient seriousness. Although frequently studied from other angles, they have not been considered as a resource for mainline theology. Yet feminist theology stresses the need to regard more seriously previously ignored and marginated traditions. These traditions can provide a valuable critique of, and different perspective for, the larger Christian community.

Marginal traditions, such as the Shakers, were often formed in reaction to a perceived distortion in established religion. From the outset of their history the Shakers criticized traditional familial structures, eventually understanding (beginning in the early nineteenth century) the devaluation of women as a crucial part of the problem. Indeed, because the Shakers recognized God as encompassing both traditionally masculine and feminine characteristics, and because they had a social structure that allowed for shared leadership between males and females, many current writers are greatly encouraged by the Shaker experience. Some commentators have been so impressed with the Shakers' courageous efforts, that they are ready to minimize whatever failures the Shakers experienced in the course of trying to live up to the ideal.[35]

Some take a more critical approach to Shaker ideals and efforts, yet still suggest that the Shakers can provide much valuable information. Rosemary Ruether, for example, is clear that the alternative relationships envisioned by the Shakers and other such groups "exist in forms distorted by sexism." Nevertheless, she understands their insights and efforts as part of an eschatological feminism that has broken forth intermittently in Christian ascetic, mystical, and monastic theology and again in the radical Protestant mystical, utopian, and millennarian sects such as the Shakers. Their heritage becomes part of our "usable tradition." She is optimistic that "their potential for aiding us in imagining a new humanity can be disclosed by subjecting each to feminist critique and bringing them together in a new relationship." When we allow "minority Biblical and Christian traditions to criticize dominant traditions, one begins to discover lost critical principles."[36]

The Shakers deserve our careful attention, then, even as we also subject them to current critical insights. Existing on the periphery of the American religious scene, they were freer to raise crucial questions about gender and God, questions that had been ignored or suppressed by mainline Christianity. From this perspective, those concerned with gender imagery for God need to pay particular attention to the Shaker experience and understanding of God. The Shakers may have discovered possibilities latent in Christianity that could aid us now.

Approaching the Shakers from this perspective encourages sensitivity to similarities in our current critique and theirs. It also promotes a nuanced but expectant approach to the theological insights they gleaned in trying to make Christianity gender-inclusive. Even if, upon close inspection, the Shakers do not turn out to be "the place just right" for contemporary feminists, they nevertheless may provide the church with valuable insights for theological work with gender-inclusive imagery and for practical work to make women's experience and values more central.

From the pragmatic view of imagery and doctrine, the Shakers are an especially valuable case study. They are significant because they preceded contemporary feminists in both theory and practice, in many ways functioning as a sort of laboratory for the investigation of gender-inclusive imagery for God. It is true (as will be discussed in chapter 2) that the Shakers did not intentionally begin as a sort of proto-feminist group.[37] Instead, they began as a millennialist community trying to live out a vision of the reign of God already begun. In the process they developed structures and theological insights—including gender-inclusive imagery for God—that challenged the traditional devaluing of women.

The fact that they did not intend to challenge or change God imagery at the beginning of their work—but that this happened in the process of pursuing their theological vision—serves as an asset to the current discussion. For if there is something inherent in gender-inclusive imagery for God that fosters more harmony and equality between the sexes, the Shaker experience should demonstrate this. The Shaker experiment should give us some indication of the extent to which gender-inclusive imagery for God is, per se, influential on behavior and attitudes. Equally important for the current discussion, a study of the Shakers may suggest what conditions encourage such a radical shift in the symbol system.

The content of the Shaker gender-inclusive God image is crucial, for the Shakers explored many of the options available in gender-inclusive imagery. Because this was done from within the symbol system of the Christian tradition, the Shakers are especially intriguing today. The Shakers show in what ways the symbols lend themselves to different interpretation and in what ways the symbols inherently provide parameters. For even as dissidents, the Shakers could not help being a part of their culture. Examining them helps demonstrate to what extent a protest movement can extricate itself from the reigning cultural ethos to develop another view and yet show how it is nevertheless constrained.

Fortunately, the Shakers produced and preserved a voluminous body of writings, both theological and personal, through which their religious perceptions, their daily lives, and their attitudes toward self, God, and society can be viewed. As members of an intentional community, the Shakers were able to achieve a consistency in daily life that conformed closely to the symbol structure through which they perceived reality. Their work thus is congenial especially to the contemporary concern with the integration of belief and practice, concept and experience. As such, the Shakers provide an excellent source of data from which to examine some of the outlines and implications of gender-inclusive imagery for God.

But the Shakers also are particularly intriguing because they began their work on gender and God so unselfconsciously. They did not set out to develop male and female images of God because they thought it would improve relations between men and women. Rather, they began with a millennialist vision of the realized reign of God. It was in the service of such a vision that an exclusively male-imaged God was found inadequate.

CHAPTER TWO

THE DEVELOPMENT OF
THE SHAKER IDEA
OF GOD

C ontemporary feminist theology places a high value on several of the elements present within Shaker-ism, such as a climate receptive to female experience and influence, the intention to share authority between women and men, and especially the effort to break the hold of exclusively male imagery for God. Since God imagery has become a pivotal issue in feminist theology, the presence of gender-inclusive imagery for God in Shakerism makes the Shakers particularly attractive. However, the Shaker experience does not conform to one of the principal arguments in modern work with God imagery. The argument holds that changes in God imagery play a major role in effecting changes in experience and authority structures. In Shaker history, the reverse order applies. The experience of a woman, Ann Lee, and then the institution of shared authority both preceded the theological development of gender-inclusive God imagery.

The Early Shakers and Their View of Christ and God

The idea of a gender-inclusive God apparently was not articulated in the earliest years of Shaker history.[1] Early personal remembrances of Ann Lee make no mention of it. Histories of the group do not show her teaching it. And the earliest published works by Shakers (and by their critics) do not mention it at all. Rather, millennialism was the key. The early Shakers understood themselves as the embryonic realm of God, through which the millennium would spread to all the world. They received this message in 1770 from thirty-four-year-old Lee, who for twelve years had been an active but not prominent part of a small apocalyptic group in Bolton, near Manchester, England. This group was formed in 1747 by two tailors, James and Jane Wardley.[2]

Since the group was accustomed to Jane Wardley's leadership, and called her Mother, they were predisposed to be receptive to female inspiration and leadership. According to Shaker sources, when Lee proclaimed that she had received a profound message in a vision from the Lord Jesus Christ, it is said "she was received and acknowledged as the first Mother, or spiritual Parent in the line of the female."[3] Essentially she claimed that a second coming of Christ had already occurred in her life and was possible for every follower. The millennium had arrived and would spread as people believed and were obedient to this message.

In spite of the radical fact that this message had been delivered by a woman and contained nascent—but as yet undeveloped—christological implications, it is likely that the God imagery of these earliest believers remained male. This orientation did not prevent the group from acknowledging Ann Lee as its new leader, nor did it prevent a core of them from willingly following her to America in response to her vision that the message would prosper there. Arriving in America in 1774, most of the group stayed loyal to Lee through several years of poverty and persecution and were rewarded when members began to flock to them beginning in 1779, due to the fall-out of a regional religious revival. Lee's husband had left her soon after their arrival when it became clear Lee would never abandon her insistence on celibacy.

The Shaker stress on celibacy was to become a major factor in the justification of gender-inclusive God imagery, but it did not begin from this motivation. Lee's adoption of celibacy had begun in England during the time she was married to Abraham Stanley. Although Lee's profession of celibacy may have come as a result of the Wardleys' practical advice to refrain—when Lee came to them in great turmoil over her own growing belief that sexual intercourse was sinful,[4]—celibacy was probably not essential to the Wardleys' message. It may have been her own spiritualized response to an unwanted marriage that included the loss of all four children at very young ages. In any case, celibacy did become an integral part of Lee's teaching, and the most important element of the group's perfectionistic understanding of salvation. What is remarkable is that this one woman's vision should have been so influential for so many. Celibacy remained a pivotal doctrine of the Society throughout its history, affecting in some way each of the estimated twenty thousand people who passed through its doors.

Celibacy was not an aberrant belief at that time, but was a common interpretation of Scripture among various religious groups.[5] Lee, however, felt it was a message from God, given to her after "deep mortification and suffering."[6] She declared that in a vision, Christ taught her that the root of all evil was inordinate lust, manifested in "the doleful works of the flesh."[7] Thus Lee's profession of celibacy arose out of her own personal experience, intense struggling, and what she obviously understood as an illuminating and central religious vision.

This one woman's experience had a profound effect on the two-hundred-year history of the Society founded through her influence. The Shakers interpreted celibacy as

the path to redemption, the freeing of the whole person to serve God, and the way to enter into and celebrate the new realm of God where there would be no marrying or giving in marriage. Also central to Lee's teaching was the required practice of confessing sins orally to her or a representative. Oral, private, and frequent confession, along with the requirement of celibacy, remained core aspects of Shakerism throughout its long history.

The early Shakers clearly were open to the experience and influence of this one woman, but it is unlikely that these followers saw her as the second Christ, much less as an embodiment of the female or feminine element of deity. The belief in Lee as a female Christ does not become evident in the literature until the nineteenth century and precedes the emergence of their gender-inclusive God concept. The earliest believers, instead, seem to have remembered Ann Lee as a charismatic figure who healed, counseled, elicited confessions, delivered prophetic messages, bore persecution bravely, and set an example of perseverance, loving self-giving, and spiritual fervor for her followers. Both Lee and her followers seem to have regarded her as the bearer of the new millennialist message, the inaugurator of the new era in which the Second Coming had begun in the church (the purified Shakers) as a whole. Any discussion of this period is hampered by the fact that during her lifetime neither the illiterate Lee nor her earliest followers had any of their teachings or history recorded. Lee died in 1784, but the first written remembrances of her were not published until 1816.[8] By that time many of her early followers had died, and all had had a long time to reflect on their experience with Lee and discuss it with others. These testimonies do not present a unified view of Lee's self-understanding. Few, if any, of Lee's remembered statements give the impression that she saw herself as a Christ figure.[9] Rather, her insistence that she was married to Christ, that Christ was her "head and Lord," that "it is not I that speak; it is Christ who dwells in me," and that anyone who desired could be married to Christ, do not appear to be messianic. Instead, they reflect evidence of Lee's having had a strong spiritual experience of being "in Christ."[10]

The question of Lee's self-understanding and status has often been a difficult subject for observers of the Shakers. In fact, early outside commentators on the Shakers were particularly outraged by the reverence for Ann Lee. The fact that the group was founded and led by a woman was problematic enough for many early observers. But, in addition, for anyone—especially a woman—to be seen as a Christ figure would indicate to many extreme hubris or even insanity.[11] However, the evidence of the earliest testimonies shows a woman who had a powerful spiritual experience of being united to Christ, but also one who seems to have made a definite distinction between herself, Christ, and God.

What is clear and especially significant is that no doctrine of a gender-inclusive God is expressed by Lee in this memorial literature. Both believers and Lee use male pronouns and imagery for God, seeming quite comfortable with traditional understandings of God as judge, giver of light and power, revealer of sins, desiring obedience and sacrifice. Indeed, some of Lee's remembered statements make it appear that she held a subordinationist view of gender as well as traditional God imagery.

It is understandable that Lee might condone the subordination of wives to husbands among the "world's people" since they were living in the older dispensation, for it would have counteracted the world's accusation that the Shakers broke up families. But she appears to have held the same view for married believers. Thus Lee counseled the wife of a believing couple to "be obedient to your husband . . . as the Church is to Christ: for the husband is the head of the wife, even as Christ is the head of the Church."[12]

When Lee justified her leadership of the Shakers in answer to an objection by Joseph Meacham—who cited the Pauline injunction for women to remain silent and subordinate—Lee said, "The order of man, in the natural creation, is a figure of the order of God in the spiritual creation . . . The woman, being second, must be subject to her husband, who is the first, but when the man is gone, the right of government belongs to the woman: So is the family of Christ."[13] It is uncertain whether she was referring to Christ here or to her own husband. In either case, and regardless of celibacy, she seems to have described her leadership as deriving from a male source.

The Development of Shared Authority

Not only did the experience of Ann Lee precede the formation of the Shaker gender-inclusive God doctrine, but the beginning of their shared authority did as well. This system, with its parallel lines of male and female authority, grew out of the necessity of communal living. Living in community had not been an original tenet of either the Wardleys or Ann Lee. But once in America, the early Shakers were drawn to live together for mutual support in a hostile environment. Their British origins, pacifism, and strange message—especially the profession of celibacy— made them suspect and subject to attack in Revolutionary New England. These factors, plus their early poverty, made living together a good idea. A more theologically inten- tional reason also can be surmised, for by living in community they could mutually exhort and better realize and celebrate the joy of their millennialist vision.

Men and women living together celibately created other

problems. People newly vowed to celibacy could be tempted by too close contact with the opposite sex, and the theologically essential requirement of confessing all one's sins could create special problems if confession had to be made to a member of the opposite sex. At first, oral confession may have been made to the offended party, to Lee, or to the original elders. The early group in America was largely unstructured, often on the move, and willing to obey the lead of the charismatic Lee. As the group grew, and especially after Lee's death in 1784, it became more realistic for women leaders to hear women's confessions, deal with women members' personal problems, and set the standards and pace of domestic work. Similarly, it would be less complicated and less threatening to their celibacy for men to handle their own matters.[14] But Lee herself may have set an early pattern for shared authority. The first testimonies frequently refer to her self-sacrificial model, which her followers emulated, and to her sharing leadership with a few trusted advisors. The phrase "Mother and the Elders" is frequently repeated. These elders are thought to have been her brother William; James Whittaker, a young man she had raised from childhood; Joseph Meacham, who had been a local religious leader and one of her first American converts; and possibly several others. It is not clear if this group was composed exclusively of men; there is some evidence that Lee also may have depended on a number of women.[15] However, the institutionalizing of genuine shared authority between the sexes did not happen immediately.

In spite of Ann Lee's example as chief leader, the group appointed Whittaker to lead after her death in 1784 and another man, Joseph Meacham, after Whittaker's death three years later. The official beginning of Shaker gender-parallel authority did not come until Joseph Meacham, said by Lee to be "her first born son" in America,[16] appointed Lucy Wright to serve as leader of the

Society's "women's lot." Wright had been in charge of the females at the original community at Niskeyuna during Lee's life, and some sources indicate that Mother Ann intended Wright for a central leadership role. According to biographer Calvin Green, when Lee was in her final illness she asked for Wright to nurse her, and through this period Lee tried to "gather" the feelings of the sisters to Lucy "to prepare them for what was afterwards to take place." And after Lee's death, "it was plainly seen by discerning minds, that a large portion of Mother's mantle rested on Lucy."[17] In spite of this, it took three years and the group's appointment of two male leaders before Wright got her chance to wear this mantle and then only through the decision of Meacham.

Meacham may have been trying to put into practice what Mother Ann had intended originally,[18] even over the objections of the larger body. The institution of this Gospel Order, completed in 1792, with its parallel lines of male and female authority, did present a challenge for the new society. It caused many departures from the community, and even the remaining Shakers had difficulty accepting a woman other than Lee as a leader. Green later put it this way:

> Many among believers had formerly belonged to Sects that were in this naturalistic State, & therefore had a sentiment that all females must be held to these carnal ordinances. . . . It required much travel & light in the Spirit to dissipate their former traditionated sentiments & learn the *Unity* of the *Spirit*, between male & female. Hence [Wright] . . . had great prejudice to overcome, & many erroneous ideas & sentiments to correct. . . . These things caused Mother Lucy much labor, & extreme tribulation.[19]

Former Shaker Valentine Rathbun noticed the same problem: "They acknowledged Elder Joseph to be their father in the Gospel; but as to a mother, it was such a new thing and so unexpected that there was something of a labor before the matter was finished." Rathbun wrote his account in 1800 and does not mention the Shakers teaching a gender-inclusive God concept.[20] Nor does Meacham, in the key document he wrote to explain Shakerism, relate his appointment of Wright to gender inclusivity in God. Neither does he mention Ann Lee, an indication that her importance may have declined during his administration.[21]

It also is possible that Wright had initially been appointed simply as the leader of the woman's lot, not co-head with Meacham of all the Society.[22] In any case, Wright apparently had many obstacles to overcome to get members to acknowledge her authority, even though Mother Ann had set a precedent for female leadership and may have even designated Wright to succeed her. In fact, lingering hesitancy about female leadership may have dogged Wright's entire tenure (which lasted until her death in 1821) in spite of all that was accomplished during this period.[23]

Nevertheless, for that day, the Shaker structure of Gospel Order offered many more opportunities for females to exercise leadership than was available in most other contemporary institutions. The Shakers were organized by bishoprics (a geographic area), villages or communities (several together forming a bishopric) and families (several within each village). Although occasionally members of the same biological family might be housed in the same Shaker family, quite often wives, husbands, and children who joined together were separated. Each family was composed of a group of Shaker women and men on the same spiritual level, led by two elders and two eldresses. Each bishopric was led by a ministry of similar composition. Gospel Order culminated in a head ministry, based in New Lebanon, New York, composed of two eldresses and two elders who shared governance, with a deciding say accorded to one of the four. When Meacham died in 1796, the presiding eldership passed to Wright.

Wright's twenty-five year tenure was remarkable, for she clearly presided over the zenith of Shakerism. After Wright's assumption of leadership, Shakerism entered a time of expansion that coincided with and benefited significantly from the Second Great Awakening and the Kentucky revival in the west. Wright supervised this growth and also encouraged the development of a clear testimony through theological treatises, tracts, new worship forms, and missionary forays. It was during Wright's tenure that the gender-inclusive God concept finally was articulated in theological works. It had been a slow and labored process for the Shakers to move from the acceptance of one charismatic woman's leadership, to the acceptance of women as leaders in general, and finally, under a woman's aegis, to the actual development of gender-inclusive imagery for the divine.

The Development of a Gender-Inclusive Doctrine of God

Contributing Factors

Both necessity and millennial vision enriched the soil that nurtured the Shaker concept of God. The process of working out the Shaker millennial vision had taken decades and involved a number of critical practical problems. Beyond solving the challenges that communalism presented, the Shakers were obliged to contemplate their experience. Further theological reflection became necessary as they tried to explain to prospective members and new converts their unusual practices and also to justify their focus on a female figure as bearer of the millennial vision.

The Shakers valued experience over doctrine. In fact, their public attitude toward traditional theology was one of deliberate rejection and even ridicule, insisting that "human creeds and confessions, and subtle arguments . . . in the end left their abettors . . . totally destitute of the real power of salvation."[24] Such expression of the official attitude does not imply the Shakers had no concern over the content of their beliefs and did not use theology. In fact, in spite of their distrust of traditional theology, the Shakers were compelled to analyze and systematize their beliefs in order to understand their own experience, and to explain it to others.

For them, as for other groups that profess to be creedless, doctrine was inescapable.[25] The Shakers, like all religious groups, lived under and identified themselves by certain communal norms. Although unwritten, these norms existed from their earliest days and constantly were being refined and developed. It was their experience that finally compelled them to explicitly articulate the spiritual liberation that they felt. The millennial vision that Ann Lee brought—that the second coming of Christ had already happened—required believers to re-evaluate their understanding of Christ, of God, and of their own lives.

As early as the time of Whittaker's leadership, the Shakers had begun consciously to develop a theology.[26] Experience, rather than Scripture, Christian history, or any definitive theological corpus, was always the primary source and norm. Given this emphasis, it is understandable why the Shakers produced no definitive creeds or catechisms, for they were reluctant to constrain experience within such formalized confines. Even so, there was a certain "unanimity of faith," a certain consistency and continuity in their evolving belief system.[27] In the Shakers' efforts to achieve clarity and communicability, they produced many works of formal theology, and numerous less formal journal articles, poems, tracts, and brief distillations of their beliefs for the benefit of new believers, non-believing skeptics, and inquiring prospective members.

There are several elements in Shaker thought and experience that especially contributed to the development of a gender-inclusive God concept. The fact that Ann Lee was a female bearer of divine message occasioned new connections to be made between gender and God, as well as the development of a new view of Christ's second coming. The era that she announced threw history into a new light, prompting a dispensationalist view in which old rules could be transcended. Celibacy and shared authority led believers to understand that each sex was distinct and independent, in its own order, but functioning together as the image of God. And the millennial vision undergirded it all, with the view that in this embryonic new realm of God the world's ways, including its gender hierarchy, no longer applied to them.

The Prior Development of a Gender-Inclusive Christology

The Shakers began their theological work by focusing on the role of Ann Lee, rather than on the implications of that role for their understanding of God. By the early 1800s the role of Ann Lee had become pivotal. In the various editions of the original *Testimonies,* somewhat veiled christological parallels are made to her by the early believers. By the time these testimonies were written down, early believers had had time to reflect about Lee along christological lines. The titles used for Lee, such as "Mother," "The Elect Lady," and "the Woman clothed with the sun," would have definite implications for people steeped in the biblical tradition before joining the Shakers.[28]

John Farrington compared himself to the Samaritan woman at the well and Ann to Jesus, saying "I have seen a woman who was able to tell me all that I ever did in my life."[29] Hannah Cogswell said, "She was truly a woman of sorrows, and acquainted with grief."[30] Sometimes even more explicit identifications were made, such as "I know . . . that Christ really began his second appearance in her, and dwelt in her."[31] But whether these parallels to Jesus were the product of years of reflection or already were explicit during Lee's life cannot be ascertained.

Lee's importance also can be noted through the views of apostates and ridiculers of the Shakers. As early as 1783, Valentine Rathbun, once a promising Shaker and then a famous critic, said Shakers claimed Ann Lee "is the woman spoken of in . . . Revelation . . . who was clothed with the sun. . . . Further, that she is the mother of all the elect and that no blessing can come to any person, but only by and through her."[32] About twenty years later, Thomas Brown insisted he was taught that "obedience to Ann was the only way of salvation" and that belief in her as "Christ in the female" was the "foundation principle" of the faith.[33] Thus the evidence does not prove that Lee saw herself as a Christ figure, but it does show that her followers increasingly saw her that way.

The theological significance of Lee continued to evolve throughout Shaker history. Consistent in the Shaker view was the claim that Lee was an exemplar, not a savior in the traditional sense. Neither Jesus nor Ann Lee was believed to perform any sort of substitutionary atonement. Both were human beings, albeit very sanctified ones, who had acquired their roles as exemplars through a form of divine adoptionism. Salvation was thus the choice and work of each individual believer in this perfectionistic system. To be saved required a forsaking of sin, which included embracing the cross of celibacy, plus the full and regular confession of sins.

Not every Shaker necessarily understood Lee as the female Christ, even in the sense of prime exemplar. While many did see her as the female embodiment of the Christ Spirit,[34] a view especially prevalent during the first half of the nineteenth century, for others she was merely the announcer of Christ's second appearing that actually occurred in the community of believers.[35]

Through the first three-quarters of the nineteenth century, both christological views can be found. Thus, as late as 1867 member C. E. Sears could declare that Shakers believe "the second coming of Christ must necessarily be through a female . . .[and] this event has already taken place."[36] Yet only six years later, another Shaker wrote, "Ann Lee was simply the Elder Sister in Christianity, as was Jesus the Elder Brother. They are leaders in, and representatives of, the 'new creation' on earth, and their true followers . . . are travailing to a brother and sisterhood in Christ that will make them equally sons and daughters of God with their parents."[37]

By the later nineteenth century and beyond, it is clear that Shakers had begun to disavow that they worshiped Lee in any way. The stress was moved from Mother Ann as second Christ to the gender inclusivity in the Godhead, with Ann and Jesus as the ones who make this truth clear.[38] There was a sort of bell-curve effect in the Shaker understanding of Ann Lee. During her lifetime, she worked to get her followers to realize the second coming could happen to each individual through the community of believers. But the Shaker view of her rose steadily until by the early 1800s she was seen as the female embodiment of the Christ Spirit. This view was prevalent especially during the revival period known as "Mother Ann's Work" (1837–47).

This high view of Ann Lee subsided as the Shakers began to decline numerically, until by the late nineteenth and early twentieth centuries the communitarian view again prevailed.[39] In 1910, for instance, a Shaker pamphlet complained, "Some tell us that 'the Shakers worship Ann Lee.' This is far from truth. We worship God alone. As a woman, Ann Lee was but one among millions; as an instrument to express divine truth in an inauspicious time, we revere her sincerity and marvel at her courage."[40]

The Emergence of the Gender-Inclusive God Concept

The evolution of the gender-inclusive God concept took a different route. It is not clear exactly when the Shakers began publicly professing that God was two-gendered: Almighty Power (or Eternal Father) and Holy Wisdom (or Eternal Mother). The doctrine did not receive formal theological articulation until 1808, with the publication of Benjamin S. Youngs' *Testimonies of Christ's Second Appearing.* Even in this early edition (the book was republished in 1810, 1823, and 1856), the role of Ann Lee plays a more prominent part than the idea of God as both female and male. However, the outlines of divine gender inclusivity are clearly laid in the earliest editions; by the 1856 edition they had been expanded into a lengthy section.

Following Youngs' first edition, another work, Calvin Green and Seth Wells' *Summary View of the Millennial Church* (1823)[41], also clearly outlines the gender-inclusive God concept. Youngs' explication of the two-gendered concept of God is pivotal, and continued to influence later explications of this theme. A close examination of this gender-inclusive God concept as revealed in Youngs' and several other representative works will be explored in the next chapter.

By the time of Mother Ann's Work at mid-century, the gender-inclusive doctrine of God had reached a prominence which was to continue, and in fact to grow, throughout the nineteenth and into the twentieth century. This period of Mother Ann's Work is key because at that time the Society was trying to revive its spiritual fervor, an effort that included the shoring up of the core tenets and experience of its faith. By mid-century the gender-inclusive doctrine of God had been fully formed and publicized enough to have a definite influence. In looking at testimonies of faith from this period (chapter 4), it becomes clear that these believers considered gender-inclusive imagery for God, and especially a high view of the role of Ann Lee, acknowledged aspects of their faith.

Following the revival period, the prominence of the gender-inclusive God theme seemed to rise in proportion to the decline in the stress on Ann Lee. For example, in 1860 a pastor visiting a Shaker service at Union Village, Ohio, commented on the discourse given during the meeting. The Shaker speaker explained that God is dual and that "this 'dual God' is discovered in the eternal power of God, and in the eternal wisdom of God. The former is represented by the man, and the latter by the woman." The pastor makes no mention of any teaching about Ann Lee.[42] Similarly, around 1888, Shaker writer Catherine Allen saw the main message in Jesus' and Ann's example to be that God includes both male and female, as compared with the earlier Shaker stress on Lee's inaugurating the millennium or providing the way to salvation. "The Christ Spirit . . . [that] descended upon Jesus, representing through him the Fatherhood of God, [has also descended] as truly baptized Ann Lee, representing and teaching the Divine Motherhood."[43]

The fact that the Shaker view of Ann Lee and God changed over time was not something Shakers would feel compelled to conceal. The Shakers never insisted upon ageless consistency in theological doctrine; for them revelation was progressive and history was dispensational. If differing views of Ann Lee were held over time, and even at the same time between different believers, Shakers could understand this as progress in the Society or differences in the spiritual development of individuals.

For them it was not a departure from Lee's message if later Shakers understood more than Lee had done herself. Noted Shaker writers Calvin Green and Seth Wells clearly state that "The light of Divine truth is progressive in the Church."[44] Since authority was believed to come primarily from God through the ministry, only the process, and not the content, of revelation was fixed. As for the Bible, since revelation was seen as an on-going process, cumulative and progressive, the Bible could be revered for the wisdom it contained, but surpassed whenever later revelation made that necessary.[45]

The Centrality of Worship and Experience

The key expression of the Shaker gender-inclusive understanding of God was in Shaker worship. Here men and women witnessed both to their distinctions and to their unity as the image of God. Shakers met in family groupings during the week to sing and dance their faith, then all came together in the meeting house each Sunday. Men and women entered the meeting house from parallel doors at precisely the same moment, kept together with members of their own sex, and did not come into physical contact. Yet they both sang the same songs and danced together in planned, intricate patterns that testified to their harmonious mutuality. Both men and women also had the opportunity to break out into emotional, spontaneous physical manifestations of their faith. This could include shaking, whirling, stamping, arm-waving, and other exercises that the individual felt led to perform.

During the revival period of Mother Ann's Work this aspect of worship became particularly lively and included symbolic visitations and messages from Almighty Power and Holy Mother Wisdom. Worship may well have been the secret ingredient in Shaker success. For although Shakerism disavowed the reproductive aspect of being human, the freedom of physical expression in worship may have allowed for the erotic element of human sexuality to be expressed.[46]

Perhaps it is this freedom and latent eroticism in Shaker worship that attracted scores of visitors to their open Sunday meetings. Witnessing a Shaker service became the high point on many tourist agendas, as people traveled for miles to sit in the specially provided galleries and watch the Shakers' peculiar expression of faith. Visitors' accounts of these services routinely express shock and scandal at the sight of Shaker men and women dancing, shaking, and whirling. But the Shakers endured this ridicule in order to witness to the world about the truth they believed Shakerism possessed. Shaker worship was meant to be the high point of community life, providing the key element that gave significance to the rest of their controlled lives.

When judging the relevancy of the Shaker experiment to contemporary theology it is important not to downplay the centrality of religious experience and goals. Testimonies and autobiographies reveal that, especially in the early years, it was not attraction to the unique gender-parallel social structure, but concerns over personal salvation that prompted people to join the Shakers. In the first forty years or so of their history, a large proportion of converts had been involved personally in the various religious revivals in America before becoming Shakers. Even as late as the 1840s—when a prospective member's motivation for joining the apparently stable Shaker structure, in the midst of a troubled American economy, could be as much material security as anything—religious motivations were still present for many. Few demonstrate this better than

Henry Stone, a member at New Lebanon, New York, who explained his pilgrimage to the Shakers.

> The God of the Arminian would save if he could, but *cannot*—The God of the Calvinist could save if he would, but will not—The God of the Universalist can save, and will save at some future time but they cannot tell *when* nor *how*—This much I had learned, when thirty four years of age. I had sought and prayed for salvation, this way, that and the others—I had resolved and reresolved—but it was all of no avail—no salvation came— . . . This much I say I had learned by experience . . . when by the mercy and goodness of God my mind was directed toward the people called *"shakers."*[47]

The Shakers accepted all sincere seekers, no matter whether the novice expressed joy over hearing the millennium had arrived, concern for personal salvation, or the desire for a safe and secure haven. Therefore, not every new member had to be drawn in particular to the radical Shaker idea that God was Father and Mother. Nevertheless, each would encounter and have to reconcile himself or herself to it, for by the nineteenth century this had become a central tenet in Shakerism. Given modern expectations about the influence of this idea of God, one would expect the sheer presence of this countercultural view to have had important effects on the Society. Yet history reveals that the emergence of gender-inclusive imagery for God did not produce the extensive systemic changes that modern theory suggests.

The Shakers in the Light of Current Presuppositions

For one thing, neither gender-inclusive imagery for God nor having women in leadership did away with traditional forms of government. Even with its parallel gender lines, concern for religious experience, and stress on leading through humble example, the Shaker system was relentlessly hierarchical. Although God was believed to communicate with all believers, the responsibility for discerning these "gifts," and the ultimate direction of the Society, rested with the leadership. In this sense, divine guidance flowed from the top down.

Each family in the Shaker community represented a level on the spiritual hierarchy, with the Church family the most advanced, and the Gathering Order (for newcomers) the least. Members from the respective orders were not even to speak to one another, lest the lower corrupt the higher. Any believer could theoretically work his or her way up through the ranks, based on spiritual progress, but all decisions on promotion were made by the leadership. Even the allowance for newcomers to affirm only those tenets they genuinely believed did not completely ameliorate this hierarchy.

Shaker Thomas Brown, for instance, complained to the elders before leaving the Society: "When I first came . . . I was . . . told to act according to the light I had from God. . . . But now . . . it is not as I feel, but as you feel for me; now it is no more acting according to my light, but your light."[48] Historian Priscilla Brewer tempers this criticism by stressing that "Shaker Elders and Eldresses did not seek power; if they had, they would never have been judged fit to exercise it. Meekness was the key: an understanding that they were chosen to serve God and His special people, not themselves." Brewer focuses much attention on Shaker leadership style, seeing weak leadership as one reason for their eventual decline.[49] Whether Shaker leaders were meek, weak, or truly servant-like, the critical issue is that they conceived their system hierarchically throughout their history, even after the emergence of gender-inclusive imagery for God.

Nor did the emergence of gender-inclusive imagery for God change Shaker work patterns. It is true that from the outset Shakers organized work along gender-parallel lines, with both deacons and deaconesses exercising temporal authority. But jobs were assigned according to traditional gender roles. Thus the female lot was responsible for the typical chores handled by the women of that day. Women ran the kitchens, laundries, and infirmaries, and were responsible for domestic cleaning, including tidying the brothers' rooms, and mending their clothes. Men performed agricultural work and other heavy outdoor labor.

On the positive side, women had some economic leverage, since they were able to sell the surplus of their domestic industries. There were often many children in the communities, and the symbolic import of the Shaker celibacy doctrine functioned to relieve women of exclusive child-rearing responsibilities. Shaker order meant that males and females were to stay within their respective lots. Thus among the numerous orphaned and abandoned children the Shakers accepted, as well as those children brought into the community by converts, the boys and girls were separated from each other and cared for by a member of their own sex. This practice did not hold for the youngest boys, who were cared for by women; in addition, the maintenance of the boys' clothes and all food preparation were women's responsibilities. Nevertheless, this child-rearing work was spread between the sexes, a significant factor as increasing numbers of children joined the group in the first half of the nineteenth century.

Not everyone enjoyed this arrangement. Nicholas Briggs, placed as a child among the Shakers when his mother and sister joined, complained that he missed their company and female influence in general.

> My companions from morning until night were boys. . . . They were not bad boys . . . but they seemed to me who had always

lived with my mother and sister rough and coarse. . . . How I longed . . . to spend an hour with my mother, or my sister, or some agreeable female friend. Girls sometimes wish they were boys, but I never heard a boy wishing to be a girl, yet when I saw those girls at the church, in the dining room, in the door yard, I wished I could be a girl just a little while for a change, that I might enjoy something finer than these rough boys.[50]

Briggs' experience with the Shakers occurred in the late nineteenth century, a time when the gender-inclusive concept of God had assumed prominence in Shaker teaching. The cultural stereotype of women as refined and men as coarse is clear here. The image of God as Mother partook of such gender stereotypes, as will be examined later. Yet one wonders if, ironically, it was the Shaker long-term emphasis on the high value of the "feminine element" that enabled Briggs to publicly reveal such a wish.

Nevertheless, Briggs' longing to be with his mother and sister is important to note. These feelings were tolerated in a child, but they would have been seen as a sign of deficient spiritual development. The ideal for Shakers was to reserve one's ultimate loyalty and affection for the community. Love for natural mother and father was not seen as an aid in loving God as Father and Mother, nor a step toward loving one's Shaker fathers and mothers. Instead, it was considered a hindrance. Thus, although Briggs was allowed to visit his mother, his attachment was ultimately discouraged.

Notwithstanding the freedom permitted me to visit my mother, I knew the sentiment of the people was vehemently opposed to what they termed natural relation, and they continually declaimed against it in our meetings. It was a perpetual testimony of hate for father, mother, brother, and sister.

Is it then any wonder that embarrassment invariably attended frequent visits to my mother?[51]

Briggs' Shaker experience occurred late in Shaker history, but this theme is echoed throughout Shaker literature, from the earliest published works.[52] It reveals an inner ambivalence over the nature of familial relationships since, on one hand, Shakers were meant to hate their natural mothers and fathers, yet on the other, feel love for their Shaker elders as mothers and fathers and ultimately regard God as divine Father and Mother.

In spite of the repudiation of biologically based domestic roles, Shaker women remained largely confined to those tasks society traditionally assigned women. Not only were women confined to the domestic round, but also few of them dealt as extensively with the world as men were allowed to do, since much of the itinerant selling to the world was done by the males.[53]

This concentration of the women's work indoors is perhaps what made many visitors note that the women looked pale and sickly, while the men looked ruddy and healthy.[54] It is noteworthy how often observers chose to specifically comment on the Shakers' appearance. There is sometimes a particularly peeved tone to the many negative comments by male observers, who often took great pains to call the sisters unattractive. Artemus Ward (Charles Farrar Browne), for instance, in a satirical sketch, described one sister as "a solum female, lookin sumwhat like a last year's beanpole stuck into a long meal bag." He then has her say, "Us poor wimin folks would git along a grate deal better if there was no men!"[55]

Charles Dickens was notoriously unhappy with his visit to the Shakers, where he was refused admittance to Shaker services. (They had been closed to the public during the revival period.)[56] Dickens had to content himself with visiting their store. "The stock," he said, "was presided over by something alive in a russet case, which the elder said was a woman; and which I suppose *was* a woman, though I should not have suspected it."[57] Dickens then commented that the Society is "governed by a woman, and her rule is understood to be absolute. . . . She lives, it is said, in strict seclusion, in certain rooms above the chapel, and is never shown to profane eyes. If she at all resembles the lady who presided over the store, it is a great charity to keep her as close as possible."[58] Behind the various negative comments may be outrage that these women refused to adorn themselves according to male desires, repudiated sexual intercourse, and would not participate in the cultural ethos of marital subordination. Instead they actually exercised a significant measure of their own authority.

Nevertheless, it cannot be discounted that the care and feeding of such large communities, with the greater restrictions placed upon women, could well have exerted a visibly negative effect upon the Shaker sisters. Abigail Alcott (wife of Bronson and mother of Louisa May Alcott), who was a near neighbor to the Harvard Shakers during her time at the Fruitlands communitarian experiment, commented, "There is a servitude, somewhere I have no doubt. There is a fat sleek comfortable look about the men, and among the women there is a stiff awkward reserve that belongs to neither sublime resignation nor divine hope."[59]

One factor of the traditional division of labor which did eventually change was the admission of women to the ranks of trustee. Trustees were those who represented the community's business dealings to the outside world. For much of Shaker history, legal business was transacted only by males on behalf of the Society. This represented a significant element in Shaker life as the Society came into increasing contact with the world during the nineteenth century.

Given the Shaker world view, in which contact with the world was considered a distinct disadvantage to one's spiritual progress, this restriction of women could be seen as a privilege. The actual effect was that women had little or no part in many of the crucial decisions affecting their lives, such as the expansion of markets, purchase of lands, or construction of buildings. Finally, in the late nineteenth century—a time when male membership had dropped dramatically, when consciousness had raised considerably about the effect of this restriction and, indeed, when the Shaker appreciation of their gender-inclusive God doctrine had risen—women began to function as trustees.[60]

Throughout Shaker history, celibacy always remained pivotal. Celibacy could not be abandoned with the emergence of gender-inclusive God imagery because it became the very means to justify this view of God.[61] Although the Shakers held that at base God was spirit and beyond gender, they believed that God was revealed to humankind as Almighty Power (or Eternal Father) and Infinite Wisdom (or Eternal Mother).[62] The Christ Spirit, which was not strictly part of the Godhead, also had its male and female expressions, in Jesus and Ann Lee. Celibacy on the human level demonstrated this gender inclusivity at the heart of all reality because it demonstrated and perpetuated the distinctiveness of the two sexes.

Expressed as early as Youngs' 1808 edition, this Shaker form of natural theology, "the universal law of duality," was carried through the nineteenth and twentieth centuries. For example, in 1867 C. E. Sears commented:

> In the things that are made, or the universe, from inanimate matter up to man, we see the manifestation of two great fundamental principles, viz: *male* and *female*. As God is the cause . . . it logically follows that the cause *must* be male and female.[63]

In 1904, Anna White expresses the same idea. "And God said: 'Let us make man in our image.' There is the dual, the two-fold principle. . . . Everything in nature is dual, positive and negative, or masculine and feminine. This law runs through the mineral, vegetable and animal kingdoms."[64] Although all of nature testified to the gender inclusivity at the heart of deity, celibacy best demonstrated that God's two dimensions were distinct and individual, yet one. These distinctions were symbolized most aptly, they believed, in the parallelism of the two celibate lines of male and female and the oneness in the fact that the two together constituted humankind.

But the early Shakers' proclamation of celibacy was intimately linked to a vehemence against sexual intercourse and marriage; this had the potential to work against women. Even in reacting against mainstream Christianity, Shakerism inevitably was connected to it. Western culture had long dualistically stereotyped woman as more body than mind, inherently more fleshly or weaker.[65] Thus, even though celibacy was seen as equally redemptive for both men and women, the sanctified Shaker sister could not help realizing how much further she had come and how much further she would fall if ever she began to slip. The fact that she traveled a greater spiritual distance was sometimes understood as an asset, rather than a liability, but it still gave women a greater burden to carry.[66]

Elements of gender hierarchy are reflected clearly in Shaker formative theological writings. Even though their celibacy doctrine proclaimed that the sexes were distinct and parallel, they were not genuinely equal. The Shakers were not able to expunge completely the culture's dualistic tendencies. That they made an effort to avoid it is evident, as is their belief that their views and practices were a significant improvement on the world's. But a close study of their literature (chapter 3) exposes the fact that the feminine side of God, Christ, and humankind were affected, in that order, with increasing amounts of the cultural residue of gender hierarchy.

In summary, the Shaker example addresses two aspects of the modern pragmatic-type arguments for gender-inclusive God imagery. First, the contemporary expectation that a change in a culture's primary symbols precedes and helps create social change is challenged by the reversal of this process in Shakerism. The early history of the Shakers indicates that they did not begin with a gender-inclusive concept of God, nor with the explicit intention of creating equality between men and women by sharing authority and living communally.

The model of Ann Lee was valued for the millennial message she brought and/or redemptive role that she performed, but not explicitly as a justification for elevating women to a position of equality with men. If her example and message had clearly stated this, the early problems with creating such a structure likely would have been lessened. Lee's teaching provided a belief in the liberating elements of celibacy, especially for women, and the conviction that their life-style was superior to the world's for both men and women. The dominant focus was the possibility of living millennially now.

Yet the millennial motifs and practical necessities combined to have a decisive effect. The Shaker theological agenda increasingly incorporated the implications of several key insights: the millennial vision that required all to serve God fully, the fact of a woman founder that eventually radicalized their social structure and ideas of God, and the insistence upon the freedom of celibacy that impacted both social structure and God imagery. The vision of being the redeemed people of God inaugurated by Ann Lee and the Shaker efforts to realize this in practice, pushed the Shakers toward living in community, sharing authority, and explaining God as gender inclusive.

Second, in the Shaker example it is clear that the presence of gender-inclusive imagery for God did not create the harmonious society that some modern theorists envision. Alongside the emergence of gender-inclusive imagery for God in Shakerism there existed practices that modern feminism would eschew, in particular hierarchicalism, traditional division of labor, and a theological world view that permitted the retention of many gender stereotypes. Thus gender-inclusive imagery did not challenge those views, and sometimes it even reinforced them. Although a case can be made that Shakerism offered a positive alternative for women within the context of nineteenth-century America, this alternative did not include many of the elements that modern feminists consider essential outcomes of gender-inclusive imagery.

Still, in spite of their acceptance of many cultural gender restrictions and their failure to realize even the ideals they set for themselves, the Shakers were remarkably successful in creating a haven of acceptance and mutual support. In this way, they do conform to modern aspirations. In attempting to live out their religious vision of the millennial realm of God begun on earth, the Shakers achieved an unprecedented level of gender parity and a climate hospitable to a wide diversity of people.

The Shakers provided a positive alternative at a time when American women were severely restricted, both legally and socially. A woman, no matter how poor, outcast, or burdened with the care of many children, would be welcomed as an equal into Shaker society. She would be given opportunity for advancement, healthful living conditions, the company and support of other women, and a way to get out from under the rule of her husband or father. Men, too—if they had found family life burdensome or unattractive or had made a mess of their lives—would have the opportunity to do familiar work, learn new skills, be accepted by a company of men, and have all their needs provided.

In Shakerism, racial[67] and class lines were broken down, mutuality was encouraged, and the world's competitive and materialistic impulses were successfully diminished. Both men and women could worship God freely, have their religious insights respected and validated, and play an active part in the spiritual life of the community. The sanctioning effect of gender-inclusive imagery for God worked hand-in-hand with these progressive social elements to create a tight bond between belief and social reality.

In addition, their gender-inclusive imagery for God had an inherently radicalizing effect that, over time, exerted a yeast-like action on Shakerism. As the nineteenth century progressed, the Shakers became more self-conscious and proud of their gender-inclusive understanding of God. By the close of the century, this new way of looking at God had assumed such importance in Shaker self-interpretation that it became for some Shakers almost a foundational tenet. Part of this change may have been due to the inner dynamic in the exceptional combination of shared authority, openness to women's experience and influence, and gender-inclusive imagery for God.

Another reason for the increasing role of gender-inclusive imagery in Shaker consciousness was the American context. There were a number of changes going on in American society that made the Shakers become more aware of their rich heritage. For instance, the Shakers benefited from changes in the American view of gender that made the connection between females and religion more acceptable.[68] The Shakers also responded to the attention paid to them by the emerging utopian-socialist movement that appreciated, among other things, their attention to women's conditions.[69]

In addition, Shakers were affected by the consciousness-raising effect of the growing women's rights movement, which had its American beginnings at the first women's conference at Seneca Falls, New York, in 1848. By 1867 Sears makes an assertion—astonishingly similar to the contention of modern feminists—that conceptual change precedes societal reform. In doing so, he contradicts the way the process had worked within Shakerism itself. Sears notes "the increasing interest in, and agitation of the subject of women's rights, woman suffrage, &c," adding, "But we believe that woman's true sphere can be fully comprehended only by those who recognize the fact that God is *mother* as well as *father*. The promulgation of correct views of Deity must ultimately result in the proper elevation of woman, and of a consequence, the race."[70]

When Shakers reflected on what was happening in the world,[71] they came to feel that they had been the repository of a profound truth all along. The tendency then, as with Sears, was to read backwards and assume the Shakers had been aware of and practiced equality from their beginnings. "We are able to show that all the fragmentary reforms of the outside world today, find in our home a living centre, where they are embodied as a whole in daily, practical experience."[72] Thus the "Shakers have tested the equality of the sexes in government, in religious services, and in domestic life for over one hundred years."[73] This also is linked with the gender-inclusive God concept, for in reference to some recent interest in the world in the Motherhood of God, Anna White says, "To us, the simple Shakers, this grand truth was revealed one hundred and thirty-three years ago."[74]

In spite of their continuing intellectual activity and proclamation that the full equality of women was taught and practiced by the Shakers, their formative theological doctrine of God with its gender hierarchy (examined in the next chapter) was never substantially changed. In spite of some tentative efforts to the contrary,[75] generally the literature continued to rely on traditional, sphere-oriented, and thus implicitly restrictive, views of gender. For instance, Shaker writer Antoinette Doolittle, often noted for her feminism and partnership with Shaker radical Frederick Evans, wrote in 1871:

> We recognize the law of dependency running through all created things; the lesser leaning upon the greater—the weaker upon the stronger. Man is the lawful head, and is the representative of God in the male order, the Eternal Father, and will always have the supremacy. Woman, the representative of God in the female part of Deity, Mother, must act her part as co-worker, filling her sphere.[76]

In the 1880s, prominent Shaker Catherine Allen, even though insisting that women must be coequal, hastened to add "not that woman's sphere shall ever be man's sphere; God has marked as unmistakable distinctions in her mental, as in her physical structure."[77] In defining these distinctions, she and other Shakers drew upon standard cultural stereotypes and patterns of gender relations that were far from seeing male and female as equal.

This approach continued into the next century. For example, noted Shaker writer Anna White quotes with approval a paper claiming that the main symbolic function of all women, married or celibate, is motherhood.[78] Along with increasing pride in the Shaker gender-inclusive doctrine of God, there remained cultural limitations attached to it, present from its inception. No greater role than motherhood could be envisioned for the feminine element, even though this must have caused some cognitive dissonance for these celibate women—and for Shakers in general—since human motherhood held very little value for them. Even so, the standard cultural meanings for male and female were assumed along with their hierarchical connections. This will become clear as Shaker theological treatises are examined in the next chapter.

The Shakers' growing appreciation for the gender-inclusive God concept happened as the Society was declining numerically. Even a creative understanding of God and a unique social structure could not prevent certain powerful forces from impairing the strength of the Shaker social experiment. While the Shaker doctrine of God did not cause or hasten their decline, neither could it alone prevent it.

The Society had begun its relentless, though at first barely noticed, decline soon after Wright's death through a combination of both internal and external reasons. Internally, there was increasingly inadequate leadership, laxity due to unaccustomed material wealth, the admittance of lukewarm members, and the acceptance of a disproportionate number of children. External reasons included industrialization and the declining attraction of agricultural life, decreasing competitiveness of Shaker industries, the cooling down of religious revivalism in society and, finally, the devastation of the Civil War. As the Society moved through the nineteenth century, there was a growing disparity between belief and practice, concept and experience. Religious fervor died down, rules were loosened, and accommodations were made to retain members.[79]

There are lessons to be learned from the Shaker decline, in particular the fact that doctrinal creativity and tight organization alone cannot create the spiritual fervor that keeps a religion vital. However, the Shaker doctrine of God was not simply the innocent victim of alien forces. This gender-inclusive God was not a totally new reworking of the traditional Christian understanding. Creative as it was, in many ways the Shaker God image stayed rooted in a deficient form of gender inclusiveness.

In spite of the imaginative, constructive, and admirable efforts of Shaker thinkers to deal theologically with gender stereotypes, their work contained important elements of lingering gender hierarchy. This limited and inadequate understanding of God and gender continued to color Shaker thought as the Society became more appreciative of its heritage. The modern efforts towards gender-inclusive imagery for God can gain as much from an understanding of the Shaker theological failures as from an appreciation of its successes.

CHAPTER THREE

THE GENDER-INCLUSIVE GOD IN SHAKER THEOLOGY

There is very little sustained theological reflection on the relationship of God and gender in the western Christian tradition. The Shakers, in fact, are unusual in that they made an effort to incorporate the category of gender throughout an entire theological system. Even though they did not begin to publish their thoughts on God as Almighty God (the Eternal Father) and Holy Mother Wisdom (the Eternal Mother) until the first decade of the nineteenth century, from then on the gender-inclusive God concept achieved a secure place in the Shaker theological framework. Their doctrine of God merits careful examination for it shows some of the options and difficulties in a gender-inclusive approach to God, as well as its effects on christology and theological anthropology.

The formative period for this new vision of God lasted through the first quarter of the nineteenth century. It is appropriate and valuable to focus on the officially sanctioned, published theological works of this period, for here the Shakers most elaborately and self-consciously defined their understanding of God.[1] The two major theological works that outline the doctrine are Benjamin S. Youngs' *Testimony of Christ's Second Appearing*, first published in 1808, and Calvin Green and Seth Wells' *A Summary View of the Millennial Church*, published in 1823.[2] Later editions of Youngs' work (1810, 1823, 1856) drew out and refined the implications of this doctrine of God, and other authors offered commentary as the Shaker God concept began to be used to defend and promote the Shaker faith.[3]

Although the Shaker doctrine of God includes much reflection on the feminine element and on women, its formal articulation was the product of males. There was only one exception to this, Paulina Bates' *The Divine Book of Holy and Eternal Wisdom* (1849)[4]. While her work would be significant simply because she was the only woman with writings officially published by the Society during the first half of the nineteenth century, it is especially important because she wrote toward the end of Mother Ann's Work, a time when gender-inclusive imagery was at its height.

Except for Bates, it was not until the late nineteenth century that the thoughts of Shaker sisters began to be published. Much of this later work reiterated the earlier formulation of the doctrine. Therefore, focusing on the two formative theological works will give the main outlines of the Shaker understanding of God. An examination of Bates' work will then demonstrate how a woman interpreted this theology during a period of particular openness to gender-inclusive imagery. Although Bates' work is of a different genre, since it is a type of oracular mysticism, it not only clearly reflects the formative doctrine, but also contains some significant variations on it.

It is understandable that the Shakers did not publish any major theological works until the early nineteenth century. In their first three decades in America, they were largely concerned with survival, growth, and organization. In addition, they were hostile toward traditional theology and reluctant to codify their beliefs and practices.[5] Joined to these factors was the necessity to keep a low profile with unsympathetic outsiders since the Shaker views were often shocking to mainstream church people. Only one work,

Joseph Meacham's *A Concise Statement of the Principles of the Only True Church* (1790), was published before the nineteenth century, and it did not touch on the issue of gender, dealing rather with a defense of the Shaker dispensational view of history.[6]

By the early 1800s some of the pressure was off this new sect. Internally, Gospel Order was well established, some fifteen communities with healthy memberships existed, and the western frontier beckoned with its revival harvests ripe for Shakers to glean. In the east Shakers were beginning to have a reputation as good neighbors, hard workers, and honest tradespeople. In their improved circumstances, the Shakers could now afford to bring together, systematize, and publicize their theological reflections. In addition, as the Society began to missionize the Kentucky and Ohio frontiers, the needs of that movement demanded a further development of Shaker theology.

Benjamin S. Youngs, *Testimony of Christ's Second Appearing*

The Formative Statement of the Gender-Inclusive Doctrine of God

Benjamin S. Youngs, the author of the first work dealing with gender and God, had joined the Watervliet, New York, Shaker community in 1794. In 1805, already an elder, he was in the first band sent by Mother Lucy Wright to the Kentucky frontier, along with Issachar Bates and John Meacham (eldest son of Father Joseph). Although the missionaries were successful, making many converts and starting communities, it was soon realized that there was no substantive statement of belief adequate to meet their growing theological needs. Youngs thus began his writing in 1806 at the Union Village, Ohio, settlement, after submitting the project to Wright and having it approved. Youngs is said to have had "a mind of a theological turn," but likely consulted with a number of other Shakers.[7] The product of this collaboration is a massive tome (over six hundred pages), as detailed and thoroughly systematic as any worldly theological work that the Shakers previously condemned.[8]

The *Testimony of Christ's Second Appearing* is both the first systematic theology and also the most important of the Shaker works dealing with gender imagery for God. This work set the standard for the ensuing discussion. Sometimes called the Shaker Bible by outsiders, *Testimony* was a comprehensive and authoritative treatment of Shaker theology[9] and continued to be made available well into the late nineteenth century. The main themes of *Testimony* have to do with the new dispensation that Ann Lee inaugurated, the need for confession of sins, the forsaking of the sins of the flesh to achieve salvation, the superiority of the new life to life in the world, and the necessity of strict organization and community of interests to make this redeemed life prosper.

Focus on Ann Lee is crucial to the scheme; here for the first time in print she is second to Jesus in theological status. It is the theological importance of the revelation through Ann Lee that makes the Shaker gender-inclusive doctrine of God possible. Indeed, this is the theory proposed by an apostate to explain the eventual development of the Shaker dual God concept. Although he does not refer specifically to Youngs' work, apostate William Haskett, who wrote during the formative period, insists that the theological development of the gender-inclusive God could not have happened without the prior development of a high view of Ann Lee.

Haskett sees the gender-inclusive God doctrine as a fabrication necessary to justify the role of Ann Lee. He contends:

In broaching the doctrine of a female Saviour, it was essential to cite a precedent which would lend the appearance of plausibility to the tenet; but finding none in the scriptures . . . they invented a female god, in apposition to Jehovah. . . . The delusion of believing Ann to be Christ . . . forced them to introduce a male and female God.[10]

Yet Haskett's theory is challenged by the fact that even after the Shaker dual christology receded in importance, the Society continued to hold a gender-inclusive doctrine of God, in fact to elevate this concept.

Youngs' work, from the first to the last editions, does show a subtle development of the role of Ann Lee and of the gender-inclusive God concept, even though many other parts of the book are unchanged.[11] This progression reflects the general trend in the Society towards elevating gender duality—God as composed of male and female elements—as the form of gender inclusiveness they chose.

Basic to the whole notion of God as Eternal Father and Mother is the belief that the natural world is the primary source of the revelation of divine gender inclusivity. This natural theology, first expressed in Youngs' work, became pivotal to the entire argument and was carried on throughout the nineteenth century.[12] The Shakers posited a doctrine of God based in large part upon observation of the natural world. Since the natural world was considered revelatory,[13] it—along with their religious experience—served as the theological starting point rather than any more conceptually revelational element such as transcribed vision, written testimony, or direct teaching.

In *Testimony* this concept of correspondence holds that "every thing that exists has a correspondent relation to the cause of its existence." At first Youngs says that there is only a correspondence of attributes, thus "if there was no creature, there could exist no such attribute as Creator."[14] Likewise, a mother could not be a mother without a daughter, and the same holds for a father and son. (Youngs does not discuss the relationship of mother to son or father to daughter, although it would appear that by making clear this exclusion he could effectively buttress the concept of correspondence between the same gender on different levels.)

Later he implies that not just attributes, but existence is dependent upon having a correspondent relation. Thus he says that "the very existence of *Father* depends upon *Son,* as much as the existence of *Son* depends upon *Father.*"[15] Although this concept of correspondence raises at least one important theological question, that of whether it implies a necessary creation, this issue is left undeveloped. As for Scripture, Genesis 1:27 is frequently used to defend the gender-inclusive pattern on both the human and divine levels. This passage is seen to buttress, rather than serve as source for, the Shakers' belief. The essential grounding remains firmly in natural theology.

For this reason, the Shakers call their God concept gender dual, since it posits two distinct elements or attributes in God, the masculine and the feminine. It is a form of gender inclusivity, but it is not an androgynous concept. Since the Shakers observe two distinct sexes on the human (and, they say, animal, vegetable, and even mineral) level, the distinctions of male and female are assumed to be ontological on all levels of reality, in both the earthly and the heavenly spheres. Unlike some religious views of gender, where the gender distinctions are done away with in Christ or in heaven, for the Shakers there would be no ultimate or eschatological merging of male and female.

Although female and male have their source in God, Youngs avoids saying that God is *essentially* gendered, even though a "twoness" is essential to God. God is spirit and transcends, even while encompassing, gender. Thus, Youngs presents what might be termed a binitarian God.

To do this he makes a distinction between the substance of God and the ordering of that divine substance. But this is not exactly a variation on the traditional trinitarian position of one substance and two persons. Rather, the substantial part of God, although non-gendered, is dual. And the ordered part of God expresses this duality in masculine and feminine attributes. The Shakers do agree with the Christian tradition in holding that God is beyond sexuality and gender, that there is one God, and yet that there is a plural—in this case dual—quality to the Godhead.

Youngs makes clear that God, although the source of gender, is more than gendered. Thus "neither the attribute of Father nor Son, Mother nor Daughter, existed from all eternity, but derived their existence from the Creator, by those things which actually exist in the order of the old, and new creation, which is created by the eternal Word, proceeding from an everlasting source."[16] The critical point of God's encompassing but transcending gender is not often mentioned in later Shaker writings, but it is made very clear by Youngs. In later writings there is a tendency to bypass these subtle distinctions when calling God dual and to identify the masculine and feminine elements as part of the substance of God. Even in later writings—and in spite of the Shaker use of the word dual—this is not traditional dualism, where two divine powers or principles are primarily in opposition. God is dual, and this twoness is composed on the ordered side of God in distinct and non-mixing masculine and feminine elements, but these elements are complementary and cooperative (even sharing many of the same characteristics at times), and not in opposition.

By the 1856 edition the implications of the earlier editions of Youngs' book are drawn out, refined, and the gender inclusivity of God is made more significant. *Testimony of Christ's Second Appearing* does not indicate that there is a God behind God, and God is understood to be, at the most profound level, "Supreme Intelligence." Although non-personal and non-gender-specific, this Supreme Intelligence is composed of a "Two-in-One Spirit" that combines a duality of substance, which is non-gendered, and a duality of order, which is gendered. This duality of substance expresses the firm distinctions in the essence of God's unity. By calling this duality one of substance, Youngs may have intended to avoid a simply modalistic understanding of the distinctions within God where gender attributes would simply be masks or roles assumed to perform certain activities.

On the non-gendered substantive side of this duality, God is Almighty Power (also called Divine Majesty) and Infinite Wisdom (or Holy Wisdom). Gender enters as these two aspects are set in order. Thus, Almighty Power occupies the role or throne of Eternal Father, while Infinite Wisdom occupies the throne of Eternal Mother.[17]

On the surface, the two roles or attributes of Eternal Father and Eternal Mother appear coequal. Both are integral and proceed out of the everlasting substance of the unified God. They are both called eternal in the later edition, but in the earliest edition Youngs insists that

> those attributes which men have ascribed to the Deity, are not in his Divine Essence, they are not eternal, but had a beginning, and necessarily arose from comparisons, drawn by the human mind, between corresponding objects in time. . . . [thus] the Creator in the sense of mankind, received the attribute of *Father*, from the existence of the first man.[18]

Youngs thus wavers between two essentially different conceptions of God's inner being. One posits a form of functional binitarianism (which could be termed economic trinitarianism if framed within the traditional Christian doctrine) where the two attributes are expressed at a certain point for a definite purpose. The other conception posits an essential twoness in God, where duality resides at the substantial level, that is, eternally within the unity of God.

In both conceptions although God is one, and not essentially gendered in the divine substance, gender is still closely linked to the nature of God. This point is made most clearly in the 1856 edition, where an entire section is devoted to the order of deity, but the essence of it can be found in all editions. This schema is broached, for instance, in a poem at the end of the first three editions, entitled "A short Abridgement of the foregoing Testimony." Here God is addressed as a unity throughout, for example, a "God of salvation, power and grace," the "maker." However, God's substance is dual, an Everlasting Two, defined by the essential attributes of Power and Wisdom. As late as the 1856 edition, Youngs still insists that these core attributes are derived from "plain Scripture language."[19]

The way we can view the divine duality is through these attributes and their gender connections, according to this poem. Thus "the Father's high eternal throne was never fill'd by one alone: There Wisdom holds the Mother's seat, and is the Father's helper-meet."[20] This binitarian concept of God essentially is composed of Father and Holy Spirit. It is the Holy Spirit that is given the attributes of Wisdom and Mother. As will be discussed below, the Christ Spirit is not presented as part of the Godhead, but exists at an intermediary level that is not carefully defined by Youngs.

Hierarchy Within God

There is, in all editions of *Testimony of Christ's Second Appearing,* an implicit hierarchy within this Two-in-One-Spirit God. This is not surprising, since the Shakers read their theology of gender off their perceptions of the natural world, and the subordination of women to men was simply the way things were. In the poem at the end of the earliest editions, and elsewhere in them, the Mother aspect is likened more to the Holy Spirit than to an actual counterpart to God as Father, as later developed. Since the Holy Spirit has often played a more ambiguous or amorphous role in western theology, the sense of subordination or derivation has traditional roots.[21] This is evident especially in the 1808 edition, where it is said that Jesus directly manifests the Father, but Ann Lee manifests the Holy Spirit as it proceeded first through Christ Jesus.

> And as in the fulness of time, the Father took up his abode in the Son, & was revealed and made known in and by the Son, in whom dwelt the fulness of Deity, pertaining to man's redemption, so in the fulness of time, the Holy Ghost descending from Christ Jesus, took up her abode in the Daughter, in and by whom, united in a correspondent relation to the Son, the perfection of order in the Deity was revealed . . . and the mystery of God finished, pertaining to the foundation work of man's redemption.[22]

The christology in the earlier editions appears somewhat more traditional, with a closer connection posed between Jesus Christ and the Father. In later editions, the Christ Spirit becomes more of a distinct entity, more clearly derivative of than resident in the Godhead, with parallel manifestations in both Jesus and Ann. Thus as early as the 1810 edition the quotation changes. It is now the "Spirit of God" which "abode" in the Son. In addition, the words "descending from Christ Jesus" are removed. The 1823 edition repeats this change.[23] At some points it may appear that *Testimony* is presenting a trinitarian, rather than a binitarian doctrine of God—since Jesus is discussed as the Son of God. In fact, the Christ (as manifested by Jesus and then by Ann) is never presented as part of the substance, or even the attributes, of the dual God. The Christ Spirit seems to exist on a lower level, between the dual God and the human world. In the 1856 edition, Youngs posits a somewhat gnostic-style intermediary race between the Christ Spirit and humans (although he attributes this idea to Job 38:7). Thus he says:

> Before the world or order of creation was formed, and before man was created on the earth, there existed, in the Christ element, an order of spiritual beings, male and female, designated *Sons of God,* and *Morning Stars,* in union with the Eternal Father and Mother from whose living essence they were a proceeding; and who were the prototypes of the human race.[24]

After the creation of humankind, the Christ Spirit is specially manifested in the exemplary persons of Jesus and Ann Lee.

The subordinationist element in the Godhead, the root of these parallel manifestations, remains explicit from the earliest to latest editions. "The Father is first in the order of the new creation, and the Holy Ghost is the second, the glory, wisdom and perfection of the first."[25] The female element—whether called Holy Ghost (as in 1808), or Mother (as in successive editions), and called Holy Wisdom throughout—remains the glory of the Father. That this is a hierarchical judgment is evidenced by the fact that Youngs states that a lesser and a greater exist on all levels of correspondence, with the lesser being the glory of the greater.

> Thus, by ascending from the less to the greater, it may appear evident, that as the woman was taken out of the man, and is the glory of the man, and as the manifestation of the Divine Majesty dwelt in Jesus Christ, who manifested the character of the

Father's standing or correspondent relation, and by the Holy Spirit possessed the brightness of the Father's glory; so *Holy Wisdom* was the glory and perfection in the order and correspondent relation of the Divine Majesty, and who was *as one brought up with him from everlasting.*[26]

By stressing that Holy Wisdom has resided with the Father from the beginning or from everlasting, the place of Holy Wisdom in the Godhead is secured. Yet primacy is given to the masculine element, which is not only referred to by his order name of Father rather than by the non-gender specific substantive name, but is constantly mentioned first, with Holy Wisdom spoken of in relation to him. This form of internal subordination in the order of Deity is different from what has been termed the innocent subordination of the second to the first persons in traditional trinitarian theology. For in the tradition, the idea that Christ Jesus is sent into the world and is obedient to the divine will is balanced by the assertion that the first and second persons of the Trinity are essentially coequal. The western trinitarian tradition, in spite of this safeguard, nevertheless has been interpreted in a monarchical or modalistic way, even though the Shaker binitarian idea of God is more integrally hierarchical in its primal conception.

Rejection of the Trinity

The Shaker ordering of gender elements within Deity reflects the dominant cultural gender patterns of the era. Nevertheless, the Shakers believed that their concept of God was a distinct improvement on the traditional Christian view.[27] The heart of the problem for traditional theology, they believed, was in the doctrine of the Trinity. The Shakers explicitly rejected the trinitarian understanding of God because they believed it was essentially masculinist. The poem at the end of the first three editions of *Testimony*, contends that the age of anti-Christ (that is, the entire period from the primitive church until the Shaker dispensation) was characterized by a masculine trinity:

> The monstrous beast, and bloody whore
> Reign'd thirteen hundred years and more;
> And under foot the truth was trod,
> By their mysterious threefold God:
> But while they placed in the *He*
> Their sacred co-eternal *Three*,
> A righteous persecuted few
> Ador'd the everlasting *Two*.

Testimony rejects the traditional doctrine of "three distinct personalities in Deity, all in the masculine gender" and draws upon the principle of correspondence, saying there is no analogy for the Trinity in heaven or earth.[28] The traditional doctrine is thus judged as excluding woman from her proper order at every level, making in effect a Godhead of three male persons. The rejection of the Trinity in favor of a gender-inclusive God image is responsible, Shakers believed, for giving women a higher place than they could have achieved in the world. Thus Youngs asks of the traditional formulation: "From whence this subversion of the pure law and order of God, to the exclusion of the female from her equitable right and participation with the male in the order and government of God's household, the same, as if in God, the female had no existence?"[29]

The Shakers did not fully reject all aspects of traditional trinitarian theology. The sense of God as non-gendered Spirit (termed by them Supreme Intelligence), the depiction of plurality in the divine unity, and the effort to avoid a modalistic understanding of God's attributes and activity, all have similarities to the traditional doctrine of God. Nevertheless, their insistent rejection of the Trinity forced them to describe God in a binitarian way that pushed them to reify the gender stereotypes in order to define the dual attributes of God.

Gender-Inclusive Christology

A review of Youngs' christology reveals a similar dynamic between the impulse toward equality that Shaker gender parity provides and the undermining effect of the Shaker ordering of the male and female elements. This impulse toward equality is not so evident in the first edition—where the Christ is somewhat more closely identified with Jesus than with Ann—but by the 1856 edition a clear distinction is made between the Christ Spirit on one hand, and Jesus and Ann as the male and female human manifestations of that Spirit on the other. For Jesus, as for Adam, it was not good for the man to be alone; he needed a partner.

Therefore, just as Adam and Eve were necessary for the work of generating the human race, so both Jesus and Ann were needed to start the work of regeneration. There must be a spiritual Mother, as well as a spiritual Father. Ann Lee therefore is hailed as the Second Coming of Christ, the completor of the work of salvation, the one whose work allows the millennium to begin. She reveals Holy Wisdom, just as Jesus Christ reveals God the Father. Youngs' understanding of Ann Lee as a sort of co-redemptor accords her a high place in his theology.[30]

Despite this, the masculine element is declared the head on all levels of reality, even for those redeemed in Christ. Although Jesus, like Ann, was simply human in body and soul, he was made (or became) Christ Jesus, the Lord. But the First Born Woman, Ann Lee, is not the Lord (or the Lady), even though in later Shaker theology she does manifest the Christ Spirit. Instead, she is the glory of Jesus the Christ as he is the glory of the Father. In spite of the fact that, according to the Shakers, the Son of God is not eternally begotten, or God, or equal with the Father, he still is accorded a higher place than the Daughter of God, Ann Lee. Thus the standard outsiders' interpretation of Ann Lee—that she was the second Christ or Christ in the female—seems to imply the Shakers held a firmly gender-equal view of redemption. The elevation of Jesus over Ann Lee in the Shaker belief system repudiates that interpretation.

Nor does the fact that the Shakers have a "low" christology—indeed eliminating any atoning work by a human-divine figure—work to elevate women. Thus even though the Shakers have reduced the reliance on a male figure, and have included a female counterpart, this does not ultimately elevate the female to an equal status with the male. As the Shakers demonstrate, dethroning a male saviour does not automatically create gender equality.

View of Woman

In fact, it is because the Shakers believed that woman sinned first that they needed a gender-inclusive christology. This is why the full redemption of the human race could not be achieved by Jesus Christ and had to wait until the First Born Daughter had done her work. Consistent throughout all editions, this explanation holds that

> it was . . . necessary, that Christ should make his second appearing in the line of the female . . . because in the woman the root of sin was first planted, and its final destruction must begin where its foundation was first laid, and from whence it first entered the human race.[31]

This statement is qualified by saying that the man sinned equally and avoids saying that the woman was inherently more sinful, but the ordering of male and female is nevertheless evident elsewhere by the use of a traditional explanation of the Fall, that the woman sinned because she usurped the man's authority, rather than letting him lead her.[32]

But Youngs tries to avoid linking woman more closely to the flesh, an error that he ascribes to traditional theology. Given the decisively lower place accorded to the flesh in Shaker cosmology, such a linkage would seriously have compromised their concept of the feminine. In fact, it is unusual for a group that claims a form of sexual hierarchy and also makes a sharp flesh/spirit dichotomy to refrain from linking women more closely to the flesh.

In the last edition, Youngs contends that both the world and the Christian church put the woman in an impossible bind. For on one hand they praise the woman for her feminine and physical attributes, while on the other they label her more sinful because of them and thus exclude her from the government of the church. In doing this, the man actually keeps a way open to gratify his own sinful nature. Thus "proud and fallen man with vain and fleshly applause, and for no other than his own sinful purposes, worships and adores the woman, and extols her even above himself."[33]

But then, he says, traditional Christianity turns on the woman by setting up false creeds, chief of which is the doctrine of the Trinity, to prevent the woman from participating in the work of redemption. This exclusion of woman from any participation "in the order and government of the 'house of God,' " implies that "the female form[s] no part of likeness of the Divine Being." In that case, she has no purpose except to "remain a servile subject to the sinful desire and lusts of man"; she is thus "still under the 'curse' " and in fact serves as "the 'broadway' of sin and destruction, of carnal pleasure and ruin . . . [for] fallen man."[34]

Ultimately the Shaker reluctance to declare woman inherently more fleshly, while yet declaring that she is inherently weaker, provides only minimal, if any, advance over the traditional views. In their view of gender and the Fall, the Shakers partake of traditional theological justifications for sexual hierarchy. These are not altered substantially either by the fact that the Shakers claimed a woman leader in which the Christ Spirit distinctively dwelt, or by a concept of God that encompassed both genders.

Calvin Green and Seth Wells, *A Summary View*

The next significant work in the formation of the Shaker doctrine of God is *A Summary View*, written by Calvin Green and Seth Youngs Wells and published in 1823.[35] This book was produced at a pivotal time in Shaker history. In retrospect, it can be said that the seeds of the Shaker decline already had been sown. Mother Lucy Wright recently had died (1821), and no subsequent leadership of the Shakers would ever equal her strength and guidance. A crisis in leadership was beginning, members were less fervent than their forbears, and more children (who often left once they reached maturity) and less committed adults were among the new members.[36] But the repercussions of these negative factors would not become evident for years. For the Shakers of this period, it was a time of great confidence and hope. Western communities still were being formed, material security had been realized, membership was rising, and new worship practices were being developed.

Authors Green and Wells were prominent Shaker elders. Green, who had been a Shaker since infancy, was a notable preacher at the New Lebanon, New York, community and knew Wright well enough to later draft her biography. Green was especially important in the promulgation of Shaker doctrine, for he made two tours (in 1807 and again in 1810 when he carried the new edition of *Testimony* that he had helped edit) to the various societies explaining gender-inclusive christology and its further theological implications.[37]

Wells, who had been a schoolteacher before joining the Society, had been appointed by Wright as head of publications and superintendent of Shaker schools, where he introduced many innovative changes. In addition, he was a nephew of Youngs, having come to New Lebanon in 1799 to visit his uncle. Wells had been so impressed that he persuaded his parents, nine siblings, and some ten other relations to convert, thus reeling in many "gospel fish" for the Shakers.[38] Both of these men spoke from secure positions of authority and influence.

Since these two leaders had a hand in the later editions of Youngs' *Testimony*, it is not surprising that their view on gender is consistent with Youngs'. Yet *A Summary View* makes clearer the ordering within the Godhead. It is based on the theory of the male element as source or origin (a traditional Christian interpretive theme in part connected to the Genesis creation accounts, especially Genesis 2:18ff) and functions to place woman closer to sensuality and, therefore, sin. Also *A Summary View* has a more apologetic tone and is briefer, making it more accessible to the average believer and inquirer. Green and Wells agree with Youngs that God is both infinite and invisible but can only be known through divine self-revelation, "not to the learned Theologist, immured in the deep recesses of philosophical speculation."[39] They hold that the foundation for the gender-inclusive God concept is in natural, not abstract or conceptual, theology. They, too, depend upon the correspondence concept, agree that male and female have their source in God,[40] and identify these divine elements as Power and Wisdom.

Allocating the Attributes Within God

However, they go further in elaborating the meaning of these two divine elements. The main role of *"Power* [is] to create, and . . . *Wisdom* to bring forth into proper order, all the works of God." The sense of *source* as the key role of the masculine element in the Godhead comes through clearly.

> The Almighty is manifested as proceeding from everlasting, as the *first Source* of all power, and the *fountain* of all good, the *Creator* of all good beings, and is the *Eternal Father;* and the Holy Spirit of Wisdom, who was the *Co-worker* with him, from everlasting, is the *Eternal Mother,* the *bearing Spirit* of all the works of God.[41]

In a way similar to traditional trinitarian theology, where the Son is not created but eternally begotten and pre-existent from all eternity, the female element in the Shaker Godhead is from everlasting, and co-worker with the Father, especially as Wisdom. She is identified with the Holy Spirit, who is known traditionally as life-giver, and she is given the stereotypically feminine and physiologically derived attribute of birth-giving or bearing. This conflates some of the traditional trinitarian attributes of Son and Spirit, where the Spirit proceeds both from the Father and the Son (for example, Western Christianity's "filioque" concept).

But Green and Wells did not connect the life-giving attribute in the female element with the process of divine creation by calling the Eternal Mother the Creator. Rather, the Father is the Creator. Thus, in *A Summary View* the process of giving life was delineated by attributing to the Father the creating power and to the Mother the nourishing and bearing ability. This is coupled with the wisdom she possesses to direct this life into its proper order, that is, determining its sex and status.

What is evident is that the Shaker gender-inclusive God

concept includes a mixture and adaptation of disparate elements from the surrounding culture. They borrowed aspects of traditional Christian explanations for the allocation of attributes in the Godhead (but now adapted to a binitarian rather than a trinitarian God) and combined this with current scientific or popular notions about the processes of human birth and development. Because the Shakers consistently attributed their knowledge of the gender-inclusive God concept to God's revelation of it in nature, it is not surprising that they used popular ideas of biology[42] (i.e., understanding the sperm as a generative factor, and the female body as merely the incubator) to describe the respective gender-linked attributes of God. This was in keeping with their basic hermeneutic. For, they reasoned: "If it were not so, then man, who was created male and female, as father and mother, could not, with any propriety, be said to show forth the image and likeness of God."[43]

Rejection of the Trinity

Even though Green and Wells borrowed aspects of trinitarian theology, they, like Youngs, explicitly reject any identification with traditional trinitarian ideas. While these writers sometimes denounced the trinitarian concept of God as tritheistic, their more persistent complaint was that the doctrine is masculinist, failing to recognize the female principle in the Godhead, even though it is so clearly and divinely revealed on earth. The gender-inclusivity theme thus is used as a chief foil against their perceived opponent, "orthodox Christianity." This approach is strongly reiterated in many other Shaker writings throughout the nineteenth century. For example, N. Briggs, toward the end of the nineteenth century, says:

> This triple Deity has no illustration in this world of ours. The idea originated in the abnormal brain of some visionary

monk. . . . The male-God idea . . . is a relic of a barbarous age. . . . [It] is consistent with the belief that woman was made of a piece of man, and consequently is his natural appendage and legitimately his tool and his slave.[44]

In their own position, Green and Wells assert that "the manifestation of Father and Mother in the Deity, being spiritual, does not imply two *Persons,* but two *Incomprehensibles,* of one substance, from whom proceed all Divine power and life." They believe this is superior to the trinitarian view because the Shaker understanding "shows something essentially different from 'three distinct persons in one God' all in masculine gender, as established by a council of catholic bishops in the fourth century, and which has been the prevailing creed among their blind and bigoted followers to this day."[45]

Green and Wells' rejection of traditional trinitarian theology was partly due to a misinterpretation of the sense of person, believing it implied a distinct and independent personality or center of consciousness.[46] There is, in fact, a partial similarity between their own view and the traditional one. Their "one substance and two incomprehensibles" and the traditional "one substance and three persons" both are intended to communicate an adherence to monotheism, yet a demonstration of the divine differentiation. This is somewhat different than Youngs' understanding of an essential duality in the divine substance.

For Green and Wells the feminine and masculine elements of God are not in the fullest sense hypostases, but simply two modes of the one God. Green and Wells, more so than Youngs, describe a modalistic differentiation (that is, the two gender attributes as manifestations of the one God) or a functional or economic differentiation (that is, the two divine attributes seen as dispensations activated for purposes of creation and redemption), but not an essential differentiation as Youngs maintains.

Finally, Green and Wells describe the firm cooperation, essential unity, and necessary correspondence between the feminine and masculine elements that was central both to their understanding of Deity, and to the Shaker structuring of females and males in community. The emphasis on cooperation and community is a distinctive element of *A Summary View,* reiterated on all levels, especially the christological, anthropological, and ecclesiological. This pattern has its roots in the Godhead, for "in all the operations of God, *Wisdom* stands connected with *Power:* for without the corresponding operation of Wisdom to direct and bring forth into proper order, nothing could ever be brought to perfection." In addition, the feminine element is given some of those aesthetic qualities that, in the nineteenth century, had come to be thought of as the exclusive purview of women. Thus the work of "wisdom appears evident in the beauty, order, harmony and perfection of all God's works."[47]

Subordination of Female to Male

More can be learned about the understanding of God in *A Summary View* by reading the comments on females and males, and Ann Lee and Jesus. The overarching principle of correspondence remains, as does the primacy of the male based on his role as source. Again, the natural world shows divine revelation. Green and Wells say, "The natural world, and the things therein contained, were, from the beginning, wisely designed as figurative representations of spiritual things to come . . . but as a shadow compared with the substance."[48] The essential cooperation of male and female elements, and the female's task of completing is one of these lessons.

> The first parents of the natural world were created male and female. The man was first in his creation, and the woman was

95

afterwards taken from his substance, and placed in her proper order to be the second in the government and dominion of the natural world, and the order of man's creation was not complete till this was done. For it must be acknowledged by all, that without male and female, the perfection of man, in his natural creation, must have been less complete than that of the inferior part of the creation, which was evidently created male and female.[49]

However, not only do Green and Wells assert that the woman was the first to sin, they add that she may have passions more debased than the male. Thus her sentence (i.e., pain in childbearing) was "directed against her conception" because God "dispenses punishment according to the nature of the offense." Green and Wells are inconsistent here because the man, who they contend also is guilty of inordinate passions, and who even sins by enforcing his way upon the woman, receives a sentence (for example, the cursing of the ground) that is not specifically directed against his sexual sins.[50]

What results is the implication that a predilection towards fleshly sin is something the woman bears in greater measure than the man. This implication arises not only because Green and Wells do not give an explanation for the apparent discrepancy in the sentences, but also because of their earlier statements about the woman's passions. However, they stop short of making an explicit ontological assignation of "materiality," in contradistinction to spirituality, to the feminine element. Instead, woman is seen as second, as more closely associated with a stereotypically feminine, physiological quality, and yet not as an evil element. Given the Shaker dichotomy between flesh and spirit, this shows a measure of restraint on Green and Wells' part from making this connection; but, in effect, the difference between this view of the male-female relationship and the more traditional dualistic view is minimal.

Gender-Inclusive Christology

The same themes are reiterated in Green and Wells' christology. The "spiritual union between male and female," as observed in the true church of Christ, both points to a higher reality and also receives its power from that spiritual union that exists "in the head of that body, which is Christ." Such a correspondence *must* exist on the level of soteriology, for if the divine Spirit appeared in one man, should it not "also appear in a woman, and distinguish her as a leader, and an example of righteousness to all women?"[51]

Still, her function as completor, exemplar, and correspondent to Jesus is not the only reason that God raised up "that chosen female in whom the second appearing of Christ first commenced."[52] For God's soteriologic plan could not be completed until a woman had been "endowed . . . with the power to effect the deliverance of lost man from the bondage of sin, and to usher in the latter day of glory."[53] The reason this must be a woman is a two-edged sword. For Eve

> was the first to violate the temple of chastity, and to lead mankind into the work of generation . . . and by this means corrupted the work at the very fountain; so a female, who was the natural offspring of the first Eve, and under the same loss, was the proper character to be empowered to break the charm which binds mankind under that loss, and to take the lead in coming out of it.[54]

View of Woman

The female element of God's human creation is placed in closer proximity to sin by this line of reasoning. Yet, as near as this comes to identifying woman more closely with the flesh, Green and Wells cannot go that far. If they had identified a distinctly ontological taint in woman, it would have been difficult to explain Ann Lee's ability to be in the divine Mother's image and to receive the Spirit of Christ and manifest it. For "the image and likeness of the Eternal Mother was formed in her, as the first-born Daughter, as really as the image and likeness of the Eternal Father was formed in the Lord Jesus, the first-born Son." Lee is thus "the true Bride of the Lamb, and the first Mother of all the children of Christ." The "Spirit of Wisdom in Christ" could only be truly manifested when "she was revealed in the female, as a Mother *in* Christ."[55]

The relationship between the Eternal Mother and the Eternal Father, between Ann and Jesus, and between female and male, each has its proper order, and this repeatedly counteracts any elevation of the feminine element. In answer to the question, Why was not Ann Lee born of a virgin? Green and Wells state Eve was taken out of Adam, "therefore she was dependent on him, and it was her duty to be subject to him as her head and lord." They fall back on the traditional hierarchical source-based argument that there can only be one head, one authority, for: "Had the woman been created in the same manner that the man was, there would have been two separate heads of the creation; and as neither of them could have had the pre-eminence; so neither of them could have been placed in a state of subordination to the other." The same pattern holds on the christological level "so that Divine Spirit with which the second woman was endowed . . . was taken from the Spirit of the Second Adam, the Lord Jesus Christ; therefore she was necessarily dependent on him, was subject to him, and always acknowledged him, as her head and lord."[56]

In spite of this subordinationist theme, Green and Wells believe that the Shaker spiritual union between males and females was a decided elevation for the woman from her place in the natural world. They state that this union is a reflection of higher truths and as such cannot be perceived by non-believers, who do not "seem to know any other design in the creation of the female, nor any other essential use for her than that of carnal enjoyment in a sexual union, and the production of offspring through that medium."[57] Despite their feelings of superiority, the Shakers' elevation of the female cannot be said to be egalitarian. The stress on source roles and hierarchy prevails. More than Youngs, Green and Wells put a great emphasis on the secondary role of the Eternal Mother, the secondary and subordinate role of Ann Lee, and the secondary, subordinate, and weaker role of the female.

In conclusion, both Youngs' *Testimony*, and Green and Wells' *A Summary View*, together provide the formative view of the gender-inclusive God concept. Both works present God as a unity, incomprehensible, and beyond gender specificity, yet expressed in masculine and feminine principles that are revealed to humans through their own biological condition. The core of the masculine principle is Almighty Power and the core of the feminine is Eternal Wisdom. The respective divine attributes are based, in large part, on the notion that the male is the source of fetal life, while the female is the receiver of this seed, its bearer and nourisher.

Unity of derivation, yet subordination of female to male, is accepted as ontological in both works. The Shakers contend, nevertheless, that their recognition of the female principle in God (and on the corresponding christological and anthropological levels) is a distinct advance over traditional Christian theology, which the Shakers believed had no positive female imagery at all. The beneficent outworkings of this improved theology, the three authors suggest, could be seen in the valued role Shakerism accorded women. Also stressed is the complementarity of the male and female and the loneliness and incompleteness of the male element before the emergence of the female.

Ancillary to this in both works is an attack on the low status accorded women by the world, and a declaration that the lot of women is much improved by Shakerism because of the group's implementation of this revelation. Yet these authors do not hesitate to hold women more culpable for the sensual nature of the first sin, stopping just short of declaring woman ontologically more fleshly. They imply that as a secondary element, woman is weaker and thus more vulnerable to the strong temptations of the flesh. She serves, they contend, as a gateway for the exercise of male fleshly propensities. The suffering of womanhood, especially in childbearing, is sometimes seen by these writers as an appropriate divine retribution for the woman's original leadership in sensuality. The Shaker profession of celibacy is, of course, reinforced by the position.

It is noteworthy that, although the gender-inclusive God concept was formulated in these two formative texts, the male authors did not seem to draw particular strength or validation for their own ministry from this gender inclusivity, or from female imagery for God. Rather, they were impressed by it, often appreciative, and they frequently used it as a weapon against their opponents. A sense of justice and pride is conveyed, but little use is made of affective language to express individual gratitude, or personal relationship to the female principle in the Godhead. For Paulina Bates, the only published female Shaker writer in the first half of the nineteenth century, personal appropriation of female divine imagery was clear at the outset.

Paulina Bates, *The Divine Book of Holy and Eternal Wisdom*

Both the context and the genre of Paulina Bates' work, *The Divine Book of Holy and Eternal Wisdom*, published in

1849, are quite different from those of the previous two texts. This is a work of oracular mysticism, but it is linked to the previous books in several ways. First, it was sanctioned and authorized by the head ministry; as such it represented an officially approved point of view. Second, although Bates claims not to have read much theological or other literature, her writings clearly show the influence of the formative Shaker theological publications. Thus, even though *The Divine Book* is not organized or presented in the manner of a systematic theology, it nevertheless contains very definite positions on God and gender.

Both Calvin Green and Seth Wells helped edit this book for publication. For Green, at least, it was a transforming experience. In his autobiography Green relates that at first he resisted this assignment from the ministry because he felt the book was unorganized, unclear, and would require extensive editing to make it understandable to the uninspired. But through a spiritual experience his mind was changed. He reports having a vision of a beautiful woman who embraces and kisses him. He is told, "this is Holy Wisdom . . . she has come to anoint you to help prepare that book which must be prepared as her testimony." Green later understands Holy Wisdom to defend the fact that males will be responsible for editing messages given to the female line. The reasoning is, he says, that the improving of deficient language and the organiz- ing of subject matter is a task "more adapted to the male sex."[58] Apparently Bates herself was not consulted when clarification was needed during the editing task, since Green believed he was inspired for this work. It is noteworthy that Green's personal encounter with, and inspiration by, the female aspect of Deity occurs at this point, since he evidenced no clear personal appropriation of the female divine in his earlier work, *A Summary View*.

The Divine Book in its entirety represents messages

inspired by Wisdom, the female aspect of God. The work is a compilation of visions, admonitions, and exhortations received by Bates beginning in 1842 during Mother Ann's Work, but not published until 1849 after much of the revival had died down. It was the second Shaker book published in this genre, the first being Philemon Stewart's 1843 work, *A Holy, Sacred, and Divine Roll and Book.*[59] Even though Stewart's book receives more attention from scholars, Bates' writings are more focused on God imagery and also more consistently theological, "a more sustained and coherent work."[60]

Bates and the community understood this as a set of oracles sent from God, often channeled through well-known Shaker spirits, angels, or other divine messengers, and delivered to Bates as the accepting medium. These writings thus carried a high degree of authority. As such, they are a significant and rare resource in which to examine the concept of God as it was interpreted by a woman during the Mother Ann's Work revival period, the height of gender-inclusive God imagery.

Bates had been brought to the Shakers as a child. At the time of the writing she was in her mid-thirties. Although a relative of prominent elder and western missionary Issachar Bates, she did not hold a high position in the Shaker hierarchy as did Youngs, Green, and Wells. That an ordinary member's work could become important is in keeping with the tenor of the period in which she wrote. During the revival period, persons of little authority and experience often achieved prestige by acting as instruments, or channels, of divine messages. The revival had begun in 1837 when several young girls in the Gathering Order of the Watervliet community began to shake, whirl, and relate visions of angels and spirit travel. This activity soon spread throughout the whole Society as Shaker visitors and letters circulated through the communities, attesting to this new work.

The revival began spontaneously and involved many rank-and-file members, but the leadership soon became involved when they recognized an opportunity to reverse the laxity and diminished fervor that had pervaded the Society following the death of many of the original Shakers. There had been other revivals in the history of Shakerism,[61] but this one was the first both to be internally focused and to stress the reception of spirit communications. This revival also went through a series of stages. It began with the physical exercises, visions, and trance states that erupted mostly among the young believers. Then it moved on to the reception of inspired messages by mediums, or instruments, messages that demanded correction for laxity, as well as offering encouragement and comfort.

Finally, the revival culminated in the reception of particular gifts, new rituals and, most important, several spiritualistic visitations from the gender-inclusive Godhead. Since the revival worked at first to enliven believers' faith, it was extended long past when it might naturally have died down. As late as 1847 the leadership still was proclaiming new spiritual gifts to arouse and stimulate members. This prolongation and increasingly extreme behavior caused an element of weariness and cynicism to arise that prompted many members to depart.[62] Nevertheless, many of the Shakers during this period were sincere and simple believers who received new hope and faith from Mother Ann's Work. In their testimonies of faith, many stress gratitude at being present "in this great day."

The writing of Bates' book (1841–1843) happened during a period of particularly unusual behavior. The new manifestations included the reception of spiritual gifts (imaginary presentation of food, clothing, and decorative objects from the spirit world), visits from spirits of Native

American Indian and other cultures, with younger believers adopting the appropriate (i.e., stereotypical) behavior, the inauguration of purification rituals (such as the clearly domestic-influenced "cleaning" and "sweeping" gifts) and outdoor "mountain meetings," and the reception of spirit drawings and new songs and dances.[63] The meetings became so unpredictable and extraordinary that the leadership closed them to the public from 1842 to 1845. The description of this behavior by Hervey Elkins, who had been a Shaker from age fourteen to twenty-nine, makes the Shaker desire for privacy at this time understandable.

> Turning rapidly upon the toes, bowing, bending, twisting, and reeling like one a victim to the fumes of intoxication; swooning and lying prostrate with limbs stiff and unyielding, like a corpse, and to all outward appearance the vital spark extinct; then suddenly resuscitating . . . and rising to join in the jubilancy around the throne of God, singing extemporaneous anthems and songs . . . such are the many exercises, effusions of devotion and supernatural illapses, of which the exposure of sin, designating, and in some cases, the transgressor, the act, and the place of perpetration, of which the accused was most generally found culpable.[64]

This background perhaps explains why the ministry waited until 1849 to publish Bates' work and included a very labored preface. The elders go to great lengths to emphasize and praise Bates' humility and childlike, passive receptivity. Bates' gender must also have played a part in their reasoning, for this stress is not present in other sanctioning statements for previous works of theology by males, including Stewart's book, which is also a work of oracular mysticism.[65] The elders say that Bates is

> a person of common natural abilities, having had a very limited privilege in letter learning . . . possessing no natural element or taste for the practice of writing; an unpretending,

unaspiring person. . . . She would often . . . beg our prayers to God for divine wisdom and support, saying that she had not the least knowledge or idea of the subject she should be required to write upon. . . . [She] conducted herself in a meek and exemplary manner . . . manifesting her love to God by simple and child-like obedience to his commandments . . .[and] has been merely as an instrument, a pen in his own hand.[66]

In *The Divine Book* Bates also portrays herself as a passive instrument of Wisdom, merely a transmitter of God's word. The inspiration of Wisdom is understood to be behind every message, and the order in which the various personae deliver them in Bates' work is significant. It follows a hierarchical pattern corresponding to the Shaker understanding of the order of revelation. Thus "the dispensation of Christ's second appearing, is properly the revelation of the Mother Spirit in God and Christ. . . . Therefore, it is proper to place the revelations of Holy Wisdom in order after the first appearance of Christ."[67] The Shaker dispensational view of history now has been extended to include the revelation of the order of Deity, whereas previously it related primarily to the christological and salvific order. Earlier ages are excused for not recognizing the feminine aspect of God, as the time for this revelation had not yet come.[68]

Clearest Explication of Hierarchy

While she reiterates many earlier themes, Bates' work is significant for its clearer explication of hierarchy. Both unity and hierarchy are shown to exist in the Godhead, but the latter element is stressed. Thus, although hierarchy was always an essential factor in Shaker theology, Bates puts more emphasis on it by showing its source and its purpose in the doctrine of God. God the Father says, "How would my body appear without a head? and how would it be led? Would not one member rise up against another, with equally as much propriety as did the body rise against the head? Truly . . . would the body become dissolved and divided against itself, and fall."[69]

God's oneness is maintained by insisting that both the Father and Eternal Wisdom together comprise that unity,[70] and that the title Lord expresses that unity of Power and Wisdom.[71] But Bates' focus is on order. It is clear that Wisdom is a lesser power and in subjection.

> This I the God of heaven decreed when I stretched forth with my almighty hand, and brought forth the lesser power, the bright and adorned Wisdom, who is as one brought up at my side, the glory of the greater power, yet subject in all things.[72]

In *The Divine Book* Bates gives the clearest exposition of hierarchy in the Godhead yet encountered in the Shaker theology surveyed. She does not present a sort of Arian subordinationism, where the second person—in this case Wisdom—is not fully God. Rather, she describes a form of functional or economic binitarianism. The different aspects (Wisdom and the Christ Spirit expressed in Jesus and Ann) share a common generic character and proceed from a primal source, but this source only contains them in essence. They are not expressed or activated until they are needed to do a certain work. Only from that moment on do they become permanent expressions.

Bates' view is in accord with the one proposed by Green and Wells. Not only is Wisdom the lesser power, but also there was a time when she was not. At a certain point she was extrapolated or drawn out of God. The editors of Bates' book elaborate: "It evidently appears that there was a period when Eternal Wisdom, the female principle in Deity, was brought forth and set in her distinct order as the Mother and bearing Spirit of all the works of God."[73]

Therefore, Bates contends that the *essence* of the eternal Mother and Father principles was present in the first source of all existence, but it appears that the dominant masculine principle had to draw out the feminine principle from himself. Although God created the heavens and the earth, "He remained alone without a helper meet in her distinct and co-operative order." This was not good, for "his glory and happiness could never be completed until the Mother Spirit was brought forth, and set in her proper order; which is his glory, and ever will be through the endless ages of eternity."[74]

The fact that this message comes from the feminine Holy Wisdom makes the pronouncement more significant, for Wisdom presents this theological position, however hierarchical, as an assertion of her worth, necessity, and rightful place in the Godhead. Again, the Shakers believe that this subordinate position is a distinct improvement.

> Men are willing to believe in a God of the male order; they are willing to believe that there are myriads of Angels; but all in the male order; willing to believe in Lucifer or Satan, a fallen angel; but in the male order; willing to believe in a Savior of man; but alone in the male order.
>
> Hence ariseth the belief in many, that the female is not in possession of a living soul; but merely a machine for the use and benefit of man in this terrestrial state of existence. And this is not to be wondered at, so long as even those who have hope of eternal life, acknowledge no other agency, either good or evil, except in the line of the male only.[75]

As with Green and Wells' work, Bates continues the theme of hierarchy on the christological and anthropological levels. Although Ann Lee is the true representative of the Eternal Mother,[76] and "they who see the Daughter, see the Mother of all,"[77] she is subordinate. Jesus and Ann are a mirror-image of the order in the Godhead for, "How then is the son of man to appear in his glory, except he appear in and with the woman, whom I created to be the bright glory of man, yet subject in all things?" On the human level Bates stresses the "bewitching influence" and "delusive charms" of woman and thus her instrumentality "in leading man into loss."[78] While not quite declaring the woman ontologically more fleshly, Bates shows her to bear much blame for the Fall and to be more responsible for fleshly sins in general. Lust is not ultimately gender-specific, but women are held more responsible for its dispersion.

View of Male and Female

Bates departs from the previous writers by clearly taking gender into account in discussing evil. She declares that there is a male/female duality in evil and in good. The distinctive sin of the male, rooted ultimately in lust, is evidenced primarily in his making war. The female rates a more elaborate depiction of her distinctive sin. Women are "busily engaged to build up the kingdom of this world, which proceedeth from the lust of the flesh, the lust of the eye, and the pride of life." In addition, they are linked more closely with sensuality than are males. The oracle asks "who among the daughters of the fall have not sipped more or less at the sensual and self-pleasing fountain which originated from the father of all sensuality, and is brought forth by the mother, the beguiling and bewitching spirit of the female."[79] There is a male source of sensuality, but it is activated, brought forth, and dispersed only by the female element. By keeping within the theological bounds of order with the male element as source, Bates has managed to link women more closely to sensuality, which is considered corrupt in the Shaker system.

Bates also differs from the previous writers by stressing the greater suffering of women, especially in childbearing, and by putting an interesting redemptive twist on the culpability of woman at the Fall. First, pain in childbearing is presented as a consequence of the joint male and female sexual sins. Bates does not contend, as Green and Wells do, that this suffering was in some way a more severe and appropriate divine retribution directed at females.

Not only does Bates hold back from this traditional theological interpretation, but she also deftly turns the sins of the first woman into a reason for the second woman's triumph, and the need for women's leadership in general. It is a great blow to men's pride, she says, for them to admit the feminine principle in God and the female nature of the second coming. If men are prone to idolize women (which in itself is a proof of the female element in God, asserts Bates) and to be seduced by them, why should men not abase their human pride and mortify the deeds of the flesh by now being led by women?[80] If men have been led down the wrong path by women, why not now be led down the right one?[81]

Bates reveals more about the respective qualities of male and female in God than do the previous three authors. The format of oracles personally delivered by God and others gives ample opportunity to survey the characteristics associated with the eternal Mother and Father. Given Bates' redemptive twist to the traditional interpretation of woman's part in the Fall, and her admonitions by Holy Wisdom asserting the right of women to lead in the new creation, one might also expect a reversal or mixing of the gender stereotypes as they pertain to the masculine and feminine principles in God. But this expectation is not realized.

The biological and stereotypical attributes still pertain to their respective sources in the Godhead. The Father God is the begetter of all,[82] the judge and punisher of sinners,[83] the merciful father of the prodigal sons,[84] the bringer-forth of the Eternal Mother. The Mother God is the bearer and nourisher,[85] the comforter,[86] charitable, merciful, and tender,[87] the companion of the meek, pure, peaceful, virtuous, and sincere.[88] Occasionally these attributes are shared (e.g., when the Mother curses[89] and both punish).[90]

Using the Stereotypes to Assert Her Authority

Bates provides a redemptive twist as she uses these stereotypes in a creative way to assert the authority of her own work. Since Bates was the first Shaker woman to write a work published and sanctioned by the lead ministry, it is possible that her embracing of the self-abnegation proper to a Shaker medium, coupled with her stress on female subordination, facilitated the Shaker ministry's decision to accept and even publish her work. Although the qualities of submission and humility were seen as more appropriate to females, in fact they were ideals for all Shakers.

Since Bates wrote during a time of spiritual revival, when many of the prophesies and visions were given by women and girls, she could link several elements together to strengthen her position. Thus, to support her role, Bates relied upon the Shaker ideal of submissiveness, the traditional understanding of a prophet as God's mouth-piece, and the cultural view that women, in general, were capable of greater receptivity and passivity.

In the Shakerism of this period, Bates' strong assertion of the hierarchical ordering of the female to the male element worked in her favor. Therefore she would stress that she was "an Instrument with mortal hand bowed down with sorrow and tribulation, knowing not what she was called to write, from one sentence to another."[91] In so doing, she indirectly compared herself to the Old Testament prophets. For example, she was instructed to "eat this roll"[92] by the "holy Angel" who would "place the word of God in . . . [her] heart,"[93] and to bow down three times in each direction and then to "lick therefrom the dust whereon thou standest. And this shall be a sign to all nations which dwell in the four quarters of the earth."[94] The editors of Bates' book obviously agreed with the analogy, for they commented: "This requirement was evidently much less degrading than that required of the prophet Ezekiel."[95]

Bates was well aware that along with the lowliness of passive instrumentality comes the grand authority vested in a mouthpiece of God. The holy Angel who gives Bates messages also issues strong statements promising to safeguard Bates, to assure the validity of her work, and to punish those who doubt it. For example, the Angel attests that all these messages were written in "the sacred book of the ancient of days" and safely guarded by God's angels.

> So fear not, little one, concerning that which thou art called to write; for it hath already been recorded in this holy and sacred book, as a swift witness, either in favor or against every soul that heareth the same, with an understanding heart.[96]

Even Holy Mother Wisdom herself speaks up for the credibility of Bates' ministry, calling her "an instrument of my own choice, a female in my own likeness," thus asserting a strong identity between them largely because of gender."[97]

In conclusion, Bates clearly used her gift of prophecy in a way that firmly sanctioned gender stereotypes as ontological, yet also allowed her own authority to be recognized. This did not pave the way for other women to become full partners in the writing of Shaker theology during this period, even though the revival represented a high point for gender-inclusive imagery. It was not until the late nineteenth century, when membership numbers had dropped dramatically—especially that of males—that a few other Shaker women's writings finally began to be published.

Although the main emphases of the Shaker doctrine of God were unchanged in these later works, the writings of Shaker sisters that began to appear in Shaker journals and tracts toward the close of the century often promoted the advantages available to women in Shakerism and stressed the female principle in God. For example, Antoinette Doolittle, in 1871 protested—on the basis of this feminine principle—the injustice done to women in the world and asserted that although "Woman is not man's equal in physical strength; neither, as a general rule, is she his equal in logic and the sterner qualities of the mind," nevertheless woman "should find and fill her proper sphere, and be something higher, purer, and better than a slave to man's passions."[98]

This sphere approach to male and female indirectly had been aided by the earlier work of Bates. But while doctrinally similar to the works of Youngs, and Green and Wells, her work incorporated significant variations of the gender-inclusive doctrine. Bates reinforced the hierarchical theme in much stronger terms than her male predecessors. She did not flinch from accusing women of greater sensuality, from stressing her own lowly position, or from making hierarchy a key element of her work. But Bates also found a source for her own authority by putting a redemptive twist on the imagery.

Unlike the male writers, Bates drew authority from the female principle in God, seeing it as the divine sanction of her own work. For Bates, support, defense, and identification came from both the angel and from Holy Mother Wisdom. Yet the female divine element also served as the sanction and role model for her passivity, receptivity, and humility. This sort of dynamic between authority and submission had not been a significant justifying factor in the work of Youngs, or of Green and Wells. This difference cannot be explained by the distinction in genres between Bates' work and their work. For Philemon Stewart's book is the same type of vision report as Bates, yet it does not contain this authority/submission dynamic.

In addition, Bates was protected and her ministry accredited by God through the angel; yet she gives the impression that she did not feel competent or authorized to continue writing or to pursue the theological implications of the nearly seven hundred pages of visions she wrote. Her instrumentality was clearly a self-limiting and ephemeral thing, not an investiture with knowledge and authority to which she had access on a more permanent basis.[99]

Women had access to power within Shakerism, but Bates did not base her authority on office. Instead she relied on the reverse avenue to authority that she obtained as a lowly and passive instrument of God. Her stress on women's ontological subordination and vulnerability reinforced her own position. She did not deny that women can hold official office and, in fact, made an implicit case for this leadership based on the tenet that women, having been first to lead men into sin, should now be the first to lead them out of it. Even so, she did not emphasize the institutionalization of this authority, although it existed within Shakerism.

Bates made extensive use of female imagery as compared to the previous writers. God's maternal side was presented as consoling, redemptive, and very accessible. In addition, Bates asserted there is a female principle in the source of evil and of good. Although both the male and female principles in evil emanate lust, the female manifests this more in sensuality, while the male provokes war. This is the closest any surveyed Shaker writer came to finding in the female an ontologically greater fleshiness. Bates, of course, saw redemption for this and drew her own ordered authority from the female element in God (as, she implied, did Ann Lee and all women). But Bates' stress on female ontological subordination, her trust in lowliness as redemptive, and her strong belief in sexual order made the authority she achieved very ambiguous and, for Shaker sisters of the period, perhaps ultimately self-defeating.

Separate but Not Equal

The overall impression from a study of these three Shaker publications is that Shaker gender parity, while creative and equalizing in some ways, was held back by its focus on ordering in the Godhead, and in Christ and humankind. Whether this ordering is based on the need for one source or one authority, to insure unity within the duality that is God, it stands in the way of that full elevation of the female element that the Shakers claimed to have accomplished. In addition, the insistence that woman sinned first set up a chain reaction that almost pushed the Shakers to declare woman more fleshly than man. Since Shaker cosmology operated with a firm hierarchical distinction between body and spirit, this focus on woman as more sensual and as sinning first—even with all their insistence that man sinned equally—created a hindrance to their impulse to equalize the sexes.

The work of Youngs, Green and Wells, and Bates represents the officially sanctioned and published form of the gender-inclusive God concept in Shakerism. To study their work is to understand the ministry-approved version of gender parity and the Shaker gender-inclusive doctrine of God. Once this position was formulated and disseminated it began to exert an influence upon Shaker thought and practice. This influence was evident particularly in the period of Mother Ann's Work. Bates' book is an example of both the influence of the gender-inclusive God concept and a sanctioned version of the doctrine. As such, her book has a special status as a published and accredited work.

However, there are other writings of a less formal nature from this period that also demonstrate the interaction of this doctrine with Shaker experience. Chief among these are the Shaker testimonies of faith. These testimonies were requested by the leadership in order to have written confirmation that the radical spiritual manifestations common during the revival period were indeed of divine origin. Among the most significant of these manifestations were the multiple visitations of Holy Mother Wisdom and the Father God. Given the pervasiveness and importance of these spiritualistic rituals, plus the careful theological articulation of the gender-inclusivity theme in the published works, the wide range and variation in believers' individual appropriation of gender-inclusive imagery is remarkable. For, as the next chapter shows, many rank-and-file believers took a measure of liberty with the formal theological schema that would not have been possible for the writers of the approved published treatises.

CHAPTER FOUR

THE VISITATIONS OF HOLY MOTHER WISDOM AND GOD THE FATHER AND THE TESTIMONIES OF SHAKERS

I n 1830, the English radical Frederick Evans was impressed when he visited the New Lebanon, New York, Shaker community for the first time. Among other things, he found "faith in a Supreme Being, not as a dry unsympathizing Trinity of three male persons, but a *Dual God*—a Father, the Fountain of wisdom and power, and a Mother, the Fountain of goodness and love to humanity." Here, finally, was a place where belief and practice coinhered, he later wrote. This was a place where " 'Woman's Rights' are fully recognized, by first giving her a Mother in Deity, to explain and protect them; where equal suffrage for men and women, and equal participation in the government of an Order founded by a woman, was an inevitable necessity."[1] Evans decided to join, and eventually he became one of the most vocal exponents of Shaker gender parity.

Evans had entered the Society at an auspicious time in the history of its dealings with the gender issue. The theology of gender inclusivity had been fully formed in the last quarter century, had been widely promulgated, and was being supported by Shaker gender-parallel government and worship practices. By the 1830s not only the leadership, but the rank-and-file believers were cognizant of this principle and, in effect, surrounded by it.

For instance, Josiah Magoon lived with the Shakers for one and a half years during the height of the revival (fall 1841 to spring 1843). Since he was part of a gathering family, he would only have been told the basics of the faith. Yet he testified that he was taught "God was Power, which was the Father. Wisdom was the Mother."[2]

In addition to this ethos, which had taken decades to become widespread in the Society, in 1837 the Shakers entered a decade of revival in which gender-inclusive imagery for God reached unprecedented proportions. In fact, at the height of this revival, the Shakers experienced a series of visitations from Holy Mother Wisdom, and at least one from the Heavenly Father, which made gender imagery for God literally come to life.

These Shaker spiritual visitations preceded by several years the spiritualistic episode in the wider American culture (inaugurated in 1847 by the rappings heard by the Fox sisters), but the Shaker revival paralleled many significant economic and religious developments in mainstream America. The Shakers were well aware of these developments and could not help but be affected by them. For instance, the beginning of Mother Ann's Work coincided with the great American economic crisis of 1837 and paralleled the ensuing depression that lasted until 1844, just when the revival manifestations were beginning to die down in the Society. The Shaker system of production may have made them somewhat depression-proof, but close ties to the world through their extensive marketing activity kept them aware of and affected by American economic developments. The atmosphere of despair and panic in the surrounding culture surely made the Shakers feel better off in their chosen countercultural life-style, no matter what problems the Society might be experiencing.

Also, just preceding the economic depression, an

expectant millennialist atmosphere had been prevalent in the American religious ethos. It was a time of many socialistic experiments, especially those of Owens and Fourier; the Mormons, too, had their beginnings in this period. The Shakers were visited by many communitarians and even attracted some of them to join. Additionally, the dietary reform movement of Sylvester Graham had an influence on the Society, as some members adopted it partly because it was believed to aid celibacy (thereby creating serious dissension since not everyone agreed that animal products, tea, and coffee should be banned). Finally, the Millerite movement, which predicted the Second Advent of Christ for 1843, paralleled the key visitations by the gender-inclusive Godhead in the Shaker Society. There were many contacts between Millerites and Shakers, and the Harvard, Massachusetts, Shaker community would especially have been affected since it was relatively near Groton, one of the encampments where thousands awaited the end of the world.[3]

With all of this going on around them, the Shakers were convinced that their revival was but the prelude to great spiritual awakenings in the world. In fact, the Shakers believed that "when . . . [the spirits] had done their work among the inhabitants of Zion, they would do a work in the world, of such magnitude, that not a place nor hamlet upon earth would remain unvisited by them."[4] All of this could only add to the sense of expectancy, excitement, and fulfillment that accompanied the spiritualistic visitations from the Godhead that occurred between 1841 and 1843.

The visitations of the Godhead represent one of the most intriguing episodes in Shaker history. They came at the height of Mother Ann's Work, after the community had experienced extraordinary physical manifestations, trance states, and spiritualistic communications from deceased Shaker leaders, along with the receiving of numerous spiritual gifts and new rituals. The visitations were the culmination of this disruptive but exhilarating time in Shaker history. For the first time the female aspect of divinity, Holy and Eternal Wisdom, was hypostatized. Andrews puts it this way, in describing the prelude to these visitations given in an ascending order of spiritual messages:

> Authorship of the messages followed a definite law of development. The initial communications came from 'our Heavenly Parents'—Jesus and Mother Ann. Toward the end of the year 1838, the Shakers began to hear from their 'Spiritual Parents'—Father Joseph, Mother Lucy, and other early leaders. Then, in 1840, the 'Eternal Parents' of the order, Almighty God and Holy Mother Wisdom, in a panoply of splendor and in the most solemn utterances of all, revealed themselves to their 'chosen people.'[5]

It is noteworthy that the messages from the Shaker leaders directly preceded those from the Godhead.

The visitations followed, and in these graphic spiritual dramas that were played out in each of the communities, the Shakers took their understanding of the crucial function of religious experience, and immediate personal revelation, to its logical extreme. The pivotal belief in a gender-inclusive Godhead was enacted literally in order to create and witness to a religious experience among members.

The Visitations of Holy Mother Wisdom and God the Father

The visits of Holy Mother Wisdom were preceded by days of both literal and symbolic purification. Cleansing rituals, auricular confession, fasting, and other mortifications were deemed necessary to prepare for each visit.

Shaker villages, "so notorious for neatness, wore an aspect fifty per cent more tidy than usual."[6] A female instrument (not always identified by name in the records), selected from the community by the elders, represented the female Wisdom aspect of God. Her visit could last for several days and included searching questions put to each member, words of exhortation and/or encouragement, special blessings, and private meetings with selected groups or individuals.

At least two lengthy accounts of these visitations are preserved in the official records of Shaker communities.[7] Great care is evidenced in the format of these official accounts (e.g., they are written in an elaborate script, and have tables of contents and subheadings). In addition, mention of the visitations occurs in other official documents, and in the testimonies and reflections of Shakers and ex-Shakers.[8] These events were clearly an important part of the official Shaker self-understanding of that period.

The first visitation from Wisdom was made to the New Lebanon community in March and April of 1841. The dialogue, recorded in great detail, presents Holy Mother as visiting Zion (the Society) due to exasperation with the Shakers' disregard of her and Almighty God's warnings. This was no meek, mild, all-accepting Deity. She did show favor to certain individuals, but much of her time was spent exhorting, reproving, correcting, and warning. She set aside one period to reproach the sisters in particular, citing unequally distributed efforts in their domestic employments (she did not address the brothers separately). Elements of forgiveness, mercy, and special notice were mixed in, but this female God figure did not embody merely the softer attributes, leaving the sterner ones for the Father God.[9]

In spite of her rounded personality, Holy Mother

Wisdom was clearly an emissary of the Father. She chose her own instruments (through the intermediary work of the elders) and spoke her own messages, yet it was clear that behind all her activity was the implicit sovereign power of God the Father. For instance, when she came to place a mark on each believer, the mark was from the Father.

She said her visit "was purposed by your Almighty Father for me to do and I have brought with me the mark of his holy name. . . . From his hand I did receive to give unto you."[10] This was somewhat balanced by her saying that the mark meant that "ye are ones who have found favour in my sight, who are by your Holy Father and Mother fully accepted," as well as her affirmation that she is imparting "my blessing . . . my wisdom my strength and my power." In addition, she promised to "ever be near to help you . . .[and] . . . lead you safely and direct you in all your proceedings."[11] But in the background was the Father's sovereign will.

The account gives specific dates for each of her visits to the rest of the Shaker communities, indicating that this ceremony was of such significance that it was repeated throughout Shakerism, even, it was noted, to those affiliate members living outside the actual communities.[12] The description of Holy Mother Wisdom's visit to Watervliet, New York, noted in addition that the New Lebanon ministry traveled to be present, thus giving even more weight to the event.[13] This visitation was repeated more than once at many of the communities.[14] Special visitations were also enacted for selected groups within the Society. One special visitation by Wisdom was described by David Lamson. Lamson and his wife, Mary, both formerly of Hopedale, one of the many utopian communities of the day, lived as Shakers at Hancock from 1843 to 1845. He explained that Holy Mother Wisdom had visited Hancock in the spring of 1843 before the Lamsons had joined. But the elders decided to reenact this ritual, in order to administer this important gift to all new arrivals.[15]

It is significant that Lamson first was carefully taught the doctrine behind the proposed visitation—thus doctrine and experience were intentionally joined. It appears that the eldership was working to awaken the membership to these insights about God. Lamson related that the elder "opened to me with much solemnity the subject of this gift" stressing that the "doctrine of the existence of both male and female in the Godhead, had of late received much attention." The elder assured him he would "realize the presence of a superior power," and that "it was an immediate and special manifestation of God."[16]

Lamson and the other selected members, dressed in their Sunday best, then were brought to Wisdom. Each greeted her with seven low bows and then knelt before the female instrument and elders, repeating, "Holy, Holy Mother Wisdom! I thank thee for thy great condescension and blessing, and for thy love and mercy to me." Holy Wisdom then placed an imaginary golden band around the member's head, saying "On it is written the name of me, Holy Mother Wisdom! the Great Jehovah! the Eternal God! Touch not mine anointed." The subject again bowed seven times and expressed thanks. The sisters then were allowed to make special requests of Mother Wisdom (Lamson says nothing about the brothers being allowed to do this). They asked for such things as faith and humility. The ceremony then was ended.[17]

The marking of each member was likely the most important part of the ceremony. From a doctrinal standpoint, this ritual taught in a graphic and clear manner the gender inclusivity of both God and Christ. In a visitation at Watervliet, one sister remembers Wisdom saying to each member as she marked them:

On the right side of thy forehead I will write with my finger the
name of the Lord thy God and also my name, Holy Holy
Mother Wisdom: And on the left side of thy forehead I will
write the name of your blessed Savior and also blessed Mother
Ann's name. These names . . . will abide with you thro time
and thro Eternity if you are faithful. But if you are not faithful,
these names are to be rubbed out.[18]

Although the visitation of Holy Mother Wisdom seems to
have been the highlight of the revival period, some
visitations also were received from the Father God,
occasionally accompanied by his Son Jesus. There is much
less in the official Shaker records about these visits, but
Lamson does go into some detail. He reports a preparatory
period of cleansing, similar to the one for Wisdom, before
the visit of the Father and his Son to Hancock in June 1844.

This preparation seems to have taken a slightly different
course from that for Wisdom. In addition to the previous
preparatory elements, members were instructed to be
especially solemn, to do no lively dancing in worship, sing
no worded songs, and to kneel frequently. The singing of
wordless songs hearkens back to the original form of
Shaker worship. The stress on solemnity, plus the rarity of
the visits relative to those by Wisdom, may indicate that the
Father God was held in even more awe than the female
aspect of Deity.

For this visitation two male instruments, appointed by the
ministry, represented the male divine characters. A similar
pattern of low bows and individual attention occurred, but
the brothers and sisters received the Father and Son in their
separate orders, rather than men and women together as
Wisdom had met them.[19] In spite of the extensive
preparation, Lamson describes a poorer performance by
the instruments and more mixed reaction from the
recipients. "Some were affected to tears, others were filled
with awe and amazement, verily believing it was God who

addressed them. Others again seemed indifferent, probably having no faith in the matter."[20]

It is difficult to determine from Lamson's remarks whether the visit of Holy Mother Wisdom was received more favorably in the Society at large, or simply better enacted at Hancock. It is possible that the visit of Wisdom did generate more excitement. Much more is written in the official records about her visit, and, as this chapter later discusses, more believers testified to having powerful spiritual experiences with her than with God the Father.

If the visitations of Wisdom were presented to the members with more enthusiasm, this could be related to the fact that women were especially active in the revival period and influenced many of its procedures.[21] They in particular would have seen the visit of Wisdom as specifically affirming their place in God's order. On the other hand, Wisdom, as the Father's emissary, may simply have been seen as more accessible, of a slightly lower rank, and thus the proper divine person to carry out the Father's will.

Role of the Leadership

The writings of believers reveal that many considered the revival a high point in their faith journeys, yet some observers have judged this period highly contrived, with the leaders merely setting the stage to impress and manipulate dependent, naive members.[22] Lamson, for example, asserts, "I am fully persuaded that they [the elders] do not believe in the pretended revelations of their prophets and prophetesses. But the gift is for the common members; if they believe it, it answers its end."[23] Lamson was not totally unsympathetic to the Shakers, but his experience of the twin visitations stretched his credulity to the breaking point and convinced him and his wife to leave. He was not alone, for a significant number of members, some of whom had at one time been instruments, also chose to leave the Society during or soon after this period.

It is true that elders urged the members to unite with whatever gift was being received at the moment. Hervey Elkins, who left the Society after fifteen years, relates, "At times I was asked by the elders if I could not . . . take upon me an Indian, a Norwegian or an Arabian spirit?" The elders encouraged this behavior in reluctant members since "they regarded the inspiration of simple and unsophisticated spirits, as a stepping stone to a higher revelation." However, they also patronized those who took the initiative themselves—even if the resulting behavior was uncouth and disruptive—"because they believed [these gifts] tended to simplify and humiliate the haughty spirits of the self-exalted and vain."[24] Given the Shaker belief that revelation came directly from God through the ministry, any role the elders might play in facilitating religious experience would be considered an essential function of their responsibility as spiritual authority and guide.

Nevertheless, in spite of the majority's belief in the legitimacy of the revival manifestations and their expectant hope that it would soon spread to the world, there was a reluctance to discuss the divine visitations in detail.[25] Both during and after the revival the visitations were kept carefully concealed from outsiders. Not only were the meetings closed to the public for three years, but according to Lamson, the elders "charged us solemnly, never from any consideration to speak of this gift to unbelievers. And if we ever spoke of it among ourselves it must be in a very solemn manner."[26] In addition, later generations of Shakers recoiled from many of the manifestations of this period and even disposed of some of the manuscripts produced during it.

Role of the Instruments

During this period, few were more committed to the manifestations than the instruments. In spite of their profuse professions of unworthiness, these men and women were the true celebrities of the revival. Not only did they receive great accord and status for their role, but for a time the charismatic source of revelation was seen to come more from them than from the elders. A significant percentage of these instruments, especially at the outset of the revival, were female, relatively young, and from the lower rungs of the hierarchical structure. Elkins says:

> I have myself, seen males, but more frequently females, in superinduced condition, apparently unconscious of earthly things and declaring in the name of departed spirits, important, and convincing revelations. Speaking in foreign tongues, and prophesying were the most common gifts.[27]

These instruments were deeply rooted in Shakerism both emotionally and intellectually. Many of the "principal instruments were . . . taken into this community in childhood . . . and . . . had nothing more than a common school education."[28] In addition, obedience and humility were marks of the good Shaker. To be a faithful instrument was to be fully obedient to one's superior or lead. Thus these people were to have "gifts, visions, revelations, speak in unknown tongues, or talk gibberish; all in obedience to the elders. Obedience to the elders is the same as obedience to God."[29]

While at least one Shaker defends the authenticity of the instruments by insisting that their own "abilities were not such as to enable them to display such mighty power and wisdom,"[30] Elkins defends them by making an opposite claim. He says that they were among "the more pure, amiable and intelligent," and thus probably the least likely to "be duped and led to subject themselves to the most humiliating attitudes of body . . . [and to] blasphemously, declare the supernatural messages of Jehovah to us—the lovely companions of their affection." This unnatural behavior was not self-induced and intended to deceive, Elkins and others insist. "I have the most unequivocal evidences . . . that the declarations of those inspired beings were true . . . and superhuman." Nevertheless, he admits, "much chaff was blended with the precious wheat."[31]

Understandably, the behavior, motivations, and especially the manifestations of the instruments came under close scrutiny. Thus the elders perhaps were motivated by a desire to prevent or counteract skepticism inside and outside the Society when they called for testimonies from the membership.[32] The elders would not only perceive a need for an affirmation of the instruments' genuine faith and character, but also a witness that these manifestations were indeed of divine origin. At least one such call occurred in the later months of 1843 and early 1844; and the testimonies themselves indicate that writers are responding to a request by their leadership.[33] A journal entry at Watervliet from December 20, 1843, notes: "The brethren and sisters over the age of 16 and under 60 years have been writing their Testimonies concerning the late manifestation of God; testifying their faith and experience of the same."[34]

The Testimonies

It is significant that a large number of available testimonies from the revival period are dated from the period during and soon after the visitations of Holy Mother Wisdom and the Eternal Father.[35] These visitations likely stretched the faith of the entire community. For instruments were now doing much more than simply serving as passive vessels for spirit communications; some of them were actively representing the Godhead in their very persons. This was likely the most radical occurrence of the entire revival period, and the need for testimonies would be the greatest at this time.

A personal testimony of faith would be an especially appropriate vehicle to meet this need. For a genuine testimony of faith is not merely an assent to a set of doctrines nor, on the other hand, a contentless expression of religious experience. Rather, a testimony is a hermeneutical act, a "collision" of perspectives,[36] where an individual's life story and encounter with the divine is interpreted within the framework of a given belief structure. Here the personal and the communal meet; experience and doctrine are fused together. In addition, the movement is dynamic, as individual believers, through these acts of interpretation, sometimes also affect or change the understanding of the communal faith story.[37] Writers are active in this process, shaping the narrative in the same way as the belief structure does. This helps explain why various testimonies within a given group can be significantly different from one another.

Like many other American sectarian groups, the Shakers hoped to discern the will of God, and God's workings, in their own lives and in the events of history.[38] Individual Shakers gave testimonies, as did Puritans and Quakers before them. Whether these were oral or written, they were meant to demonstrate that the believer was truly among the privileged. Thus, they "confirmed to themselves and to their readers that they had indeed traveled the 'straight and narrow' path and that they had correctly interpreted the steps along the way."[39]

It is not surprising, then, that Shaker testimonies often followed a standard format, for this would alert listeners to the relevant material. Testimonies given during Mother Ann's Work often include brief bits of biographical data, such as birth place and date, some identification of parental background, and occasionally some details of the religious search that led to Shakerism.[40] But most important are a statement of faith in Christ's Second Appearing and a testimony to the manifestations of the period and its high significance.

Shaker testimonies and autobiographies were "usually composed some years after the author joined the Shakers" and these writings "demonstrated to the community that the author had shaped past experience to fit the Shaker mold." This mold, unlike the narratives of more mainline groups, included a protest against many of the mores and beliefs of the dominant American culture. Therefore, since a significant aspect of Shaker narrative was "the desire to illustrate Shaker theological concepts,"[41] it could be expected that the countercultural doctrine of the gender inclusivity of God would be highlighted in testimonies from the revival period, especially now that the doctrine had been fully disseminated and gender-inclusive imagery was at its height as well.

Some sixty testimonies are available from the eastern communities of Enfield, Connecticut; Harvard, Massachusetts; Watervliet, New York; and New Lebanon, New York, written during the revival period.[42] Nearly equal numbers of females (thirty-one) and males (twenty-nine) are represented. Among those who give birth dates (the majority do), ages range from seventeen to fifty-nine (with one seventy-six-year-old), with the largest percentage of writers in their thirties and forties. About a quarter of the writers had functioned as instruments and many of the others seem to feel obliged to comment on this phenomenon. All but two had been present during the entire revival period.

At least twenty-four of the writers had been Shakers since infancy or childhood, and at least ten since adolescence.[43] Therefore these writers would have been more mature and experienced believers, articulate and confident enough to take on the task of giving a testimony. [Whether they also were among the literate ones, and thus actually wrote rather than dictated their testimonies, unfortunately is not revealed in this material.] We can expect these members to have been conversant with Shaker doctrine, familiar with gender-inclusive God imagery, and witnesses to its enactment in the visitations of the Godhead. Since the vast majority of testimonies were written in 1843, these members would have recently had the experience of Holy Mother Wisdom's visit and her particular attention to them and their companions.

These testimonies are extremely valuable in achieving some perspective on the use Shaker believers made of the theology, structures, and communally organized revival events in their own understandings of God. However, we cannot expect these writers' views to automatically represent the broad, historical cross-section of Shaker believers. Not only were the testimonies written during just one phase of Shaker history and likely preserved selectively, but also these sixty testimonies represent only four eastern communities, albeit some of the oldest and most important of the Shaker locations. While these testimonies provide a window on Shaker belief in the gender-inclusive God during the revival period, they are not intended to be a representative sample of Shakerism in general. Even so, given the importance of this period, the importance of these communities, and the congruence of factors relating to the gender-inclusive God image, it is an important window through which to look and may reveal pervasive patterns in Shakerism.

The Use of Imagery

Female Imagery for God Is Sparse

Given the congruence of factors relating to gender parity, the most striking and surprising element in these testimonies is how few of them actually use female images of God. In three of the four communities the name of Holy Mother Wisdom is absent from the majority of testimonies.[44] Since this is an unexpected factor, it is worth elaborating on this absence. Out of the nineteen testimonies from Enfield (all written between December 14 and 23, 1843), not one mentions Holy Mother Wisdom. Seventeen of these writers are women. Several writers (all women) speak of the Heavenly Father briefly, and one woman mentions the Eternal Parents. But the only female imagery in these testimonies is in the often repeated formula "Jesus Christ and blessed Mother Ann." Gender inclusivity, although recognized on the christological level, does not seem to have penetrated into the Godhead in these believers' personal conceptions of their faith as reflected in their testimonies.

Of the nine testimonies (five women, four men) from Watervliet, all dated in December 1843, only two mention the female element in Deity. Yet these were written just as their sister Bates, also from the Watervliet community, was finishing the transcription of divine messages from Wisdom that were later to be published as *The Divine Book of Holy and Eternal Wisdom.* Only Phebe Smith speaks about Wisdom's visitation, saying, "Then our Holy & Eternal Mother Wisdom, did condescend to descend from her bright throne of glory, to come to earth, & poured forth her blessing like an ocean on Zion." She also mentions "our Holy & Heavenly Father, whose power is All Mighty."[45]

It is interesting and unusual that though this writer stays within the theological parameters of the doctrine, she does not here subordinate the female to the male element. Another member, David Buckingham speaks of "the hand of Holy Wisdom," but he gives his "love and gratitude to Him" who is "the fountain of all goodness . . . [and] unbounded charity, love and mercy."[46] Another brother mentions that the instruments speak "for our Eternal Parents."[47] The formulaic "Christ and Mother Ann" is frequently used, yet gratitude and thanksgiving are offered largely to the male aspect of Deity, "the Heavenly Father, the source of mercy and of all goodness."[48]

Of the nineteen testimonies from New Lebanon (seventeen men and two women), eighteen were written in 1843 (the other is dated in January 1842).[49] Not one mentions Holy Mother Wisdom, even though New Lebanon was both the governmental center of Shakerism and the site of the first visitation of the female element in Deity. It is true that a number of the writers from this community were responding to a call to testify to the divine origin of Philemon Stewart's work, just recently published. Yet Stewart's work, like Bates', incorporates the female aspect of God. Nevertheless, no testimony writers name the female in Deity.

Testimonies to Holy Mother Wisdom at Harvard

The movement of female imagery into the Godhead is evident, however, in one of the four communities—that of Harvard. Out of thirteen available testimonies, (seven women and six men), ten of them not only mention Holy Mother Wisdom, but also demonstrate great affective ties to and experience with her. Why the Harvard writers understood and related to female imagery on the level of God—rather than simply on the christological level as in the other three communities—can only be roughly surmised. The Harvard testimonies indicate a recent visitation of Holy Mother Wisdom to that community, but the other villages likely also experienced similar recent visitations. It is possible that Harvard's proximity to, and its considerable contact with, a number of utopian and millennialist ventures—such as the Fruitlands community, also located in Harvard, and the Millerite encampment in Groton—

made Harvard members more sensitive to the contemporary spiritual seeking of the world's people, and thus more appreciative of and open to the depths of the Shaker theological vision.[50] It would not be lost on the Shakers that members of Fruitlands visited the Harvard Shakers and expressed interest. As for the Millerites, the Shakers may have felt superior to them, since the Millerites never experienced the Second Advent of Christ as they expected. The Shakers, on the other hand, witnessed several spiritualistic divine visitations during the same period.

Indeed, the advent of the Shaker gender-inclusive Godhead paralleled the Millerite events. Many of the other communities' testimonies and all the Harvard testimonies were written between January 1841 and March 1845. The Harvard accounts reveal at least three visitations of Holy Mother Wisdom and one of the Father during this time.[51] The Millerite excitement was going on simultaneously. Mass Millerite meetings were held between 1840 and 1844. A large convention was held at Groton, near the Harvard Shakers, in 1840. Miller had predicted the Second Advent for late in 1843, finally revised to October 1844. The Shakers, especially the trustees, the traveling Shaker merchants, and the elders, could not help being well aware of these events and predictions.

A more internal reason for the prevalence of female God imagery in Harvard testimonies is the likelihood that certain leading persons at the Harvard society influenced members in a more spiritualist direction. Both the Myricks and the Grosvenors, two large biological families that had joined the Harvard Shakers and assumed great importance, show evidence of sensitivity to female symbolism.[52] To fully answer this significant question will require additional detailed studies of the distinctions between each individual Shaker community, for, in fact, each did have its own specific tenor and characteristics.[53]

Nevertheless, the Harvard testimonies are especially useful in revealing certain believers' affective and experiential understandings of the gender-inclusive Godhead. Not only do they speak directly of the visitations, but also, nine of the thirteen writers (five women, four men) are instruments. This represents a much higher percentage of instruments than is present among the other communities' writers. It would behoove these instruments to give as coherent and complete a testimony as possible. In addition, many had been specifically chosen to speak for Holy Mother Wisdom, but the men would not have represented her bodily in the visitations. Here, then, is an especially close look at the content of some members' experiences with the female side of God.

It is noteworthy that four of these writers are members of the same family, the Myricks. This exceptionally large family joined the Society together in 1827 and went on to assume great importance at Harvard. All four of the Myrick siblings who wrote testimonies (Daniel, Lucy, Elijah, and Samuel) were instruments who either spoke for and/or described an intense experience with Holy Mother Wisdom. As long-term members who went on to become leaders at Harvard, they wrote from a position of respect and authority. Lucy Myrick died at age twenty-seven soon after writing her testimony, but these brothers and other Myricks later became elders at Harvard. Their parents were said to have brought some twelve children into the community, and the name Myrick is found throughout the Harvard records. The members of this family may have exerted considerable influence on their companions as they spoke so passionately about their experience with Holy Mother Wisdom.

In the Harvard testimonies, unlike those of other communities, more than half (eight) of the writers maintain a careful balance in their mention of the male and female aspects of God, using such formulas as "the Heavenly Father and Holy Mother Wisdom" or "God and Holy Mother Wisdom." Here, as in the other communities' testimonies, the term God often refers to the male aspect of Deity. The Harvard writers who testify before the 1844 visit of God the Father give more detail on Holy Mother Wisdom, though they also acknowledge the Father's existence and power. Those who write after the 1844 event compare the two visitations.

Elijah Myrick speaks only briefly about Holy Mother's purging of sin and marking of each individual. But he elaborates with great feeling on her comfort, compassion, and giving of joy, thus relying more heavily on nurturant attributes when using female imagery. "She truly turned our sorrow into joy, bound up the broken hearted, strengthened the weak, and comforted the strong nor did she leave anyone comfortless but showed a spirit of compassion & anxious desire for our prosperity in her holy work." This affected him personally and deeply: "She poured forth a fullness [that] was so sensibly felt, and so deeply engraven on my heart, that language would fail to express what I then felt."[54]

Samuel Myrick felt unworthy when called to be one of Wisdom's instruments. Since he notes that five males and seven females were called, it is clear that men as well as women were considered able to speak for the female aspect of God, if not to represent her bodily in the visitation. He did not feel able to be her instrument, but it was not because of the gender difference. "When I considered the importance of my calling—the weighty responsibility & accountibility . . . it caused me to bow low and pray earnestly to my Eternal Parents that I might be able in the fear of God, and in obedience to the will of his *anointed* lead on earth to fulfill my calling."[55] Samuel, as do most others, adheres to the theological point that the Father is the divine source, although the Mother is fully part of God.

Daniel Myrick, also an instrument of Holy Mother Wisdom, had an especially physical reaction. He says he had a

> holy and sublime feeling upon my soul and body even to that degree that for several days and nights together I could neither eat nor sleep but little but I felt strength and unnatural energy to perform my daily avocations. This feeling was throuout my whole Soul and body as much as if I had been charged with electricity—Yet all was serene and solemn without any of that temporary excitement of feeling always painful to be bourn and which impairs rather than strengthens . . . and I as well know it was an effect and a power not of my own producing for I was too cold and natural to be moved by any artificial or religious excitement.[56]

Each of these men felt inadequate to the task of representing the Mother God—this was typical of all instruments, regardless of gender—and each accepted it and had a powerful, personal experience. In addition, the range of attributes given this female image was broad. Nevertheless, each man ultimately related the work back to its source in the male aspect of Deity.

For the women writers, both at Harvard and elsewhere, expressions of unworthiness—expected of all Shakers, especially instruments—were often more self-abnegating and servile. Susan Channel, who came to the Harvard Shakers at the age of five with her mother, felt unworthy to be a Shaker, marveling that God "has, in his tender mercy and loving kindness, noticed such a poor unworthy creature." She also feels inadequate to be "Holy, Holy, and Eternal Mother Wisdom's" instrument. "There was not a partical in me that I felt prepared or worthy to receive, or communicate her word to any of her dear children."[57]

Other Shaker women relate such feelings as being like "a poor frail worm of the dust."[58]

The Harvard women, like the men, had powerful experiences of Holy Mother Wisdom. Susan Channel at first "feared and trembled lest I should miss the blessing, and of receiving her holy mark." But she exclaimed afterward, "O can any soul that has felt the forgiving spirit of our Holy Mother Wisdom, and shared in her favor and blessing, and tasted the powers of the world to come, ever give away to feelings of unthankfulness."[59]

Mary Ann Widdifield gave an especially holistic account of both the healing love and physical feelings, yet painful demands, that Wisdom brought.

> I have felt her holy love, yea my soul was filled to overflowing. I sensibly felt her presence. . . . I stood ready to obey her word regardless of my own feelings; and I have passed thro scenes of sorrow to do her holy will. But I have felt fully rewarded . . . for her love is like healing balsam to the wounded soul. Her ways are ways of pleasantness and all her paths are peace.[60]

Both Widdifield and Channel contrasted the visitations of Wisdom and the Father. Widdifield made Wisdom seem mild in comparison with the fierce justice-demanding Father. When Wisdom visited "there was a calm, serene feeling which seemed to pervade, and it was evident to all that her Blessing rested in this place." But "our Holy Fathers Visitation . . . was truly a visitation of justice." Widdifield felt her "unworthynes to stand before Him . . . his holy spirit within me . . . burned like fire, and I felt myself arraigned at his bar of justice." This "heartsearching power" showed that the Father had finally come to set things right.

> The opperations of irresistable power upon those called to be Instruments in this work, besides the heart rending grief

137

and flow of tears which often burst forth from them when called to speak the word of God, and to administer truth and justice, together with the humility of soul which I beheld in these my dear companions, all proved to me that the Lord had a controversy with Zion.[61]

Channel tempered this with a more reasonable and merciful aspect. Although the instruments "felt deap and heavy tribulation," since the Father's "spirit was like flames of fire against sin," it was clear "that the Lord had descended to earth, to reason with his creatures, as a man would reason with his friend." She "will forever praise his holy name for his loving kindness and tender mercies, tho he call me to pass thro' the fiery furnace of affliction."[62] The Mother's work is presented by most writers as judgmental, purifying, and uncompromising, yet it is nevertheless more comforting, concerned, and nurturing than that of the stern, more distant Eternal Father. Wisdom's work also is presented as more personally empowering. Few speak of infusions of energy, strength, or physical feelings when they speak of the Father aspect of God, but both men and women are personally enlivened by the Mother Spirit.

Christological Images

A brief survey of the selection and use of christological images in the four communities shows a similar pattern of attributes. Female imagery was much more common in the christological aspects of the testimonies of all four communities. Nearly every testimony writer made some use of it, even if only perfunctorily. The pattern in its use was similar to that reflected on the level of Godhead. First, the range of attributes for both Mother Ann and Jesus were broad. And Mother Ann, more than Jesus, was portrayed as not only stern and judgmental, but also as nurturant, motherly, and empowering. In addition, both males and females were related more affectively to the female than to the male image. Thus both Jesus the Savior and Mother Ann set godly examples and proclaimed the gospel of truth, but Jesus was not often affectively experienced, as Mother Ann frequently was. This close relationship to Mother Ann occurred for men as well as for women.

James Wilson, for example, described his spiritual trials and an eating problem that he had. But he knew he would find release if "Mother [Ann] would speak or communicate sumthing . . . so I might feel her presence. . . . I thought if Mother would own me it would be worth more to me then everything else." Finally when Mother Ann spoke to him, it was "sharply." "It felt to me like the awakening power of god in my soul."[63] The female element was no passive, all-accepting person, but one who called to account.

For Daniel Sizer, his path to Mother Ann led him through various denominations, as he sought Christians who would not profess one way and live another. Finally, as an adult—having spent years in a world that understood God as male or masculine—he had a revelation of Mother Ann's role: "I saw my spiritual Mother and loved her. I saw her spirit and likeness in her children and blest it. . . . I saw that the office of a Mother was to bear children to nurse, dress, clean, feed and take care of them." As important as this experience was for him, however, Sizer was led by it "to union with the Father of all souls."[64]

In Sizer's, as in many of the testimonies, the source of authority ultimately derives from the male side of God. For many Shaker believers, the theological understanding of the male element as source was clear. While Mother Ann Lee was important, it was largely as a channel of God's grace, work, and blessing. In relation to Christ she also was described as being used by this divine spirit of God to manifest his second appearance, to serve as his messenger, and to reveal his gospel. Thomas Damon, for example, affirmed that "Christ has made his second Appearance in the woman Ann Lee,"[65] focusing on the instrumental aspect of Lee's role in Shakerism and stressing her humanity. James Mott also focused on her humanity but added her parallel status with Jesus, saying, "As respects Christs [sic] making his second appearance in the Person of Ann Lee I have not the shadow of a doubt any more than that he made his first appearance in the man Jesus."[66]

Lee's importance was so pivotal for Shakerism at this time that in many descriptions she stood on her own in the narrative, even as Wisdom displayed a measure of autonomy during her visitations. Mother Ann was said to work, to "cleanse or clear away the darkness from her children," to give faith, choose instruments, "feed hungry souls," and convey her will and mind.[67] Roba Blanchard relied on "blessed Mother Ann, who has many times fed my hungry soul with manna from above."[68]

An especially affective cluster of images, in both women's and men's testimonies, spoke of Mother Ann's children, flock, fold, garden, and happy company, showing that the writer felt content and secure to be counted among that number. Nancy Ann Blandin rejoiced that she was "one of Mothers happy company" and in a vision had "seen precious fruit, and beautiful flowers in Mothers garden."[69] And Orren Haskins asserted that "if I can be the least of Mothers flock . . . I will ask no more, but bow in gratitude for my happy station."[70] All of these images do not detract from the source role of the male element, but they do show Lee as the focal point of many believers' faith.

One especially prominent theme in the work of both women and men is a strong avowal of "I am not ashamed" or "I will not disavow." Thus believers defended the scandal of a gospel proclaimed by a woman, and the validity of the revival manifestations. Mary Ann Widdifield spoke of having felt Mother Ann's spirit during the visitation and this was so precious to her that she would "never disown her holy name."[71] Because of the frequency of this insistence, there may be more here than just an adaptation of Romans 1:16 ("I am not ashamed of the Gospel of Christ"). Instead, what is suggested is a measure of discomfort or defensiveness on the part of some believers, in reference to the manifestations that accompanied Mother Ann's Work.

This defensiveness was taken to some extremes, as various writers imagined terrible tortures, persecutions, and imprisonments for their refusal to disavow Mother's Work. Thus Orren Haskins insists "I would willingly lay down my natural life than deny the manifestation of my heavenly Parents,"[72] and Lucy Clark stoutly proclaims "rather than disown the work of my ever blessed Mother I would rather be burnt at the stake or meet death in any frightful form that could be invented."[73] Indeed, the Shakers expected the world to persecute them severely on account of Mother Ann's Work. It is likely that the radical quality of the Shaker understanding of gender added considerably to believers' fears. Although Shaker doctrine, social structure, and imagery by now strongly proclaimed a comprehensive vision of gender inclusivity, these testimonies indicate that for many believers it was not fully integrated into their faith perspectives or experience.

Writers' Distinctives

But why were some believers more likely to be positively affected by female imagery than others? It would be interesting—possibly more from a psychological than a theological point of view—to find correlations between members' gender, background, time in the community, and their choice of imagery. Some suggestions can be made in this direction. Within the range of testimonies studied, it is clear that not only women but also men could have (or just as easily not have) a strong affective tie to a female divine figure, whether on the level of the Christ Spirit or God. And this does not appear to be related to being reared by the community. Though many orphans were numbered among the testifiers (about one sixth), they do not seem to have any more experiential understanding of God as parental than do those who entered with their natural parents or chose to enter as teens and adults.

Thus while many of the orphans did testify to finding true mothers and fathers among the Shaker people, so does Angus Jennett of Watervliet who joined as a child, after getting his parents' consent. Indeed, the family feeling in Shaker communities was so strong—and the emphasis on transferring loyalty from biological family to Shaker family—that even Elijah Myrick of Harvard, who joined with his parents and numerous siblings, and lived in the same community with many of them, insisted the same thing.[74] But this affective element does not seem to have caused a greater appropriation of female imagery for God.

As far as the preponderance of male testimonies from some communities and female testimonies from others, it is not clear whether the imbalance was a function of the writing and selection process, or simply an historical accident of preservation. However, the testimonies reveal a more self-effacing attitude among the women writers (including Paulina Bates) than among the men. Further research might show whether this was a dominant expectation for women in Shakerism or only an attitude encouraged by certain communities (e.g., many of the more self-abasing statements come from Watervliet women).

Conclusions

The revival period of Mother Ann's Work was an important time in the history of the Shaker gender-inclusive God concept. The doctrine of God had been officially formulated and promulgated, it was reinforced by the gender-parallel governmental system, and expressed liturgically and ritualistically. Most significant, the visitations of the dual Godhead, especially the visitations of Holy Mother Wisdom, were regarded by the Society as momentous events in the life of Shakerism. Through both official records and personal testimonies, leaders encouraged believers to express their faith in this period and in these manifestations.

Despite the importance of the Shaker doctrine of a gender-inclusive God in the officially sanctioned and published treatises, only twelve of the sixty testimonies discussed here—most of them from Harvard—even mention the female aspect of God. Despite multiple visitations from Holy Mother Wisdom, careful catechesis, and an ethos of gender parity in Shaker structures, believers' personal statements of faith only rarely mention her, and among those who do, an even smaller number report an experiential encounter or personal relationship. When female imagery was used it was frequently restricted to reference to Mother Ann Lee. References to Holy Mother Wisdom, when they occurred in believers from communities other than Harvard, were largely formulaic rather than personalized.

Given the fact that a testimony of faith is the place where a believer's life experience intersects with the religion's belief structure, it would be expected that an understanding of God as male and female would emerge most clearly there. Since this was a major tenet of Shakerism by this period, and reinforced in many ritualistic and structural ways, it is surprising that more mention is not made of this doctrine. If, in addition, one subscribes to the current theory that doctrine heavily influences experience, the unexpectedness of the situation is heightened.

When believers did testify to a personal experience with the female aspect of Deity, they described experiences of great power, transformation, challenge, and comfort. Both men and women relate these experiences, and both genders felt called to serve as instruments for Holy Mother Wisdom's messages. However, Holy Mother Wisdom is presented as having her source in the Father God, serving as his emissary, and often displaying more of the softer attributes associated with the feminine stereotype. This is not surprising, since it conforms in large part to the description of Holy Mother Wisdom presented in the formal works of theology.

It is clear that average Shakers did not simply adopt the doctrinal perspective whole even as they were surrounded by it and encouraged to appropriate it for their own. It is ironic that the gender-inclusive doctrine of God was formulated largely by males, yet the liberty taken by many males and females was to refrain from using it. Several reasons can be suggested for this disjuncture between doctrine and experience.

First, it is true that the Shaker doctrinal works "were written by some of the most senior and trusted members of the group, and . . . the enthusiasm, faith and intellectuality of these theologians probably differed greatly from that of the ordinary members."[75] In fact, Mother Ann's Work was seen by the leadership as a way to restore the integration of doctrine and experience. Many Shakers hoped this revival would rekindle the core of Shaker faith which for many had grown cold, particularly for the members who had not gone through the early privations and struggles.

But, as Stephen Marini has said, the "symbolic process would not work coercively."[76] It was not possible to create the desired spiritual responses in members, in spite of the protracted efforts of the revival period. Perhaps Lamson was correct in suspecting that the visitations, however well-intentioned, did not arise from the spiritual experience of the leadership (or, it should be added, of the general membership), but were instead orchestrated by the leaders for the benefit of the rank and file. If an apostate could note this, perhaps even those who chose to remain perceived it and felt manipulated.

Second, despite the Shakers' holistic approach to doctrine and experience, belief and practice, they were really not so different from many other religious groups. For it is common that the highest ideals of a group are not always fully appropriated or integrated in individual members' lives. Clifford Geertz has pointed out that the level of integration between doctrine and experience can differ significantly from member to member within a given system, and can even routinely fluctuate in the thoughts and actions of a given member from one period to the next.[77] Thus it cannot be assumed that the parameters and content of the formative theological doctrine of gender inclusivity express the convictions and understandings of average believers.

The rank-and-file members had a measure of freedom in using Shaker doctrine. Even though members, and especially instruments, were expected to be obedient, there was more focus on behavioral rather than theological conformity. It was the published doctrinal works that came under the closest theological scrutiny of the leadership. Few average believers approached the erudition of the formal texts in describing their Shaker experience. But they may instead have been freer with the formal doctrine as they integrated it into, or used it to help explain, their own religious experiences. Doctrine not only helps to form, but also is affected by, experience. If then, for example, the strongly stereotypical components of the gender-inclusive God belief did not provide enough radical and inspiring content to make it sufficiently compelling to average believers (even when vividly acted out), they could refrain from using it.

Finally, it may simply be the case that the vision of a gender-inclusive God had not been taught and proclaimed for a long enough time to give believers a chance to assimilate it into their own vision of the faith. Indeed, it is clear from the testimonies from the period of Mother Ann's Work that the manifestations of the revival period, including the visitations of the gender-inclusive God, were a challenge to believers' faith.

The defensive theme of "I am not ashamed" and strong protestations to never disavow the work of Mother reveal that believers felt compelled to defend the strange occurrences of Mother Ann's Work. Believers, both men and women, even went so far as to imagine they would be physically tortured to the point of death for their firm belief that these strange happenings were truly the work of God. Perhaps even for those reared, taught, and experienced in female imagery for God, many still found it a trial to affirm this iconoclastic belief in the midst of a wider culture that thoroughly resisted it.

CHAPTER FIVE

THE SHAKERS AND CONTEMPORARY THEOLOGY

N either the Shakers nor American feminists began by making a critique of God imagery. Yet over time, many in both groups came to recognize the inadequacy of male imagery for God, and to find gender-inclusive imagery more appropriate. In many other respects, the context and content of Shakerism is very different from the experience of the modern women's movement. But the Shakers provide unexpected insights for the current discussion about God imagery. Two areas warrant special consideration: first, the development and role of imagery in respect to other aspects of Shaker life; and second, the type of gender-inclusive God imagery the Shakers used. Both of these aspects have implications for the contemporary work with gender imagery and help provide theological and practical direction.

The Role of Imagery

Conclusions from the Shaker Study

In the Shaker situation, changes in imagery and doctrine did not precede, but followed, changes in historical circumstances, group self-consciousness, and social structure. The Shakers did not develop gender-inclusive God imagery because they thought it would improve relations between men and women, or help create a better social structure. Rather, the development of Shaker gender-inclusive imagery did not emerge until after several key factors were already in place. First, the Shakers reflected upon the status of founder Ann Lee and eventually adjusted their christology in light of her life and message. Second, they simultaneously worked to overcome inherited prejudices against women in leadership—prejudices that persisted in spite of Lee's example—while they developed a gender-parallel governmental structure. Third, they moved from being an embattled loosely knit sect, to being a relatively secure marginal group on the American religious scene. It was not until these processes were well under way that their doctrine of God became gender inclusive.

In spite of all this effort, the gender-inclusive God concept that emerged does not seem to have affected widespread changes in believers' experience of God. Shaker testimonies of faith provide a window on believers' understanding and use of God imagery, and the ways they interpreted their religious experience in light of these images. These testimonies are a limited expression of Shaker experience, yet the information they provide is striking. Especially important is the fact that relatively few believers actually made much use of the gender-inclusive imagery for God that their leaders taught.

Even for those most committed to the faith, references to God in testimonies drew only moderately upon the female images which the Society's theologians had developed. And when female imagery was used it was often simply formulaic, rather than personalized. In addition, believers' descriptions of their experiences often demonstrated that they understood God as predominantly masculine. Even when female imagery was mentioned, the male element of God was understood as the primary source and authority.

This was the case despite the strong female character of the Mother Ann's Work revival period. The revival allowed for much participation by women, including the development of many rituals with a decidedly domestic flavor. By the time the revival erupted, the gender-parallel social structure and gender-inclusive doctrine of God had been thoroughly developed. In addition, the Society made female imagery for God come alive through its ritualized visitations of Holy Mother Wisdom. The Shakers deliberately connected this to their doctrinal understanding of the gender-inclusive God through preparatory instruction. In light of all this, the paucity of references to Holy Mother Wisdom in testimonies of faith from this period is striking.

This impression is not reduced by the fact that female christological imagery is prominent in many of the testimonies. It is true that the parallel work of Jesus and Ann Lee is frequently mentioned by testifiers from the four communities examined in this study. Special attention is paid to the power and example of Ann Lee's life and message. Indeed, for many this was the female imagery they used to describe their individual spiritual experiences. Yet in Shaker theology neither Jesus nor Ann Lee was a divine figure, and neither performed any kind of mediatorial work. They were fully human, even though each had been selected by God to manifest the Christ Spirit. Each Shaker believer had to do his or her own work in order to emulate these two. In addition, Shaker female Christ imagery was ultimately subordinate to, and derived its power from, a male source in God. Given this and their low christology, there was a significant theological difference between references to Jesus and Ann Lee, and to Eternal Father and Holy Mother Wisdom. Therefore, the dearth of female imagery for God cannot be ameliorated by the more copious references to Ann Lee.

There were exceptions to the sparse usage of gender-inclusive God imagery in Shaker testimonies. A number of believers, especially those from the Harvard community, used female imagery for God extensively to describe their experiences of spiritual revitalization, empowerment, and divine care. Oftentimes male imagery was not even mentioned in these descriptions, or, if it was, then only perfunctorily. Holy Mother Wisdom was understood by these believers as a source of power and personal transformation.

It would simplify matters to discover that these Harvard experiences happened as a distinct result of the visitation of Holy Mother Wisdom. Then it could be assumed that the intentional ritualization of female God imagery aided believers in appropriating these images into their personal experience. But, according to the Shaker records, it appears that all of the communities enacted these visitations within the same time period. And it was shortly after these visitations that the majority of testimonies were written in each of the four communities surveyed.

It is difficult to determine why Harvard believers were more drawn to female God imagery than were members in other communities. What is suggested, however, is that community ethos plays a key part in encouraging the use of new imagery for God. Whether the impetus behind the more extensive use of female God imagery was the influence of leading community members, or stimulation from outside events, the community setting seems to have encouraged both men and women to experience God in female form.

In addition, it appears that for the Shakers in general, community reinforcement was more important in promoting the use of new imagery than was gender. A study of all four communities, including Harvard, demonstrates no correlation between the gender of the testifier and the gender imagery they used. Men were equally as likely as women to use female Christ imagery in describing their religious experience. Likewise, among those who used female imagery for God, males were as likely as females to experience spiritual transformation and to credit that to Holy Mother Wisdom. There was no indication that more men than women saw God in primarily male terms. And, similarly, there was little evidence that women used more female imagery for God than did men.

Perhaps community ethos was more important than gender in determining use of female imagery because this imagery was so counter to the surrounding culture's understanding of God. As a countercultural value it would take much external and internal reinforcement to encourage the rank-and-file members to appropriate it. This is suggested by the extreme fear of persecution that believers reveal in their revival period testimonies, and by their defiant assertions that—if need be—they would defend Mother's Work to the death. However sheltered they might have felt by the Shaker community, they realized that Shaker beliefs ran radically counter to the world's. It took a measure of defiance and courage, even in this protected environment, to overcome personal hesitations and societal prohibitions.

But reluctance to fully appropriate female imagery also was likely because the Shaker gender-inclusive doctrine of God was still fairly new. This tenet had only been promulgated for a few decades before the revival broke out. Even though the leadership encouraged female imagery— and thus was in line with formalized Shaker teachings—the members may not have had enough time to fully adjust to it and incorporate it into their personal expressions of faith.

The fact that gender-inclusive imagery for Christ, which had been prevalent for a longer period within Shakerism, was clearly incorporated into believers' expressions of faith seems to confirm this. In addition, female christological imagery was used more readily because it could be tied directly back to a female founder who still lived in the collective memory. Indeed, it is unlikely that the Shakers would have created a gender-inclusive doctrine of God without the prior realization that Ann Lee somehow uniquely testified to and revealed divine power.

Even so, having two Christ figures was not absolutely essential to the Shaker gender-inclusive doctrine of God. Neither the earliest nor the later generations of Shakers held to a dual Christ view. In fact, during the nineteenth century, Shaker writings show a great reduction in the focus on Ann Lee while at the same time female imagery for God was retained and expanded. Thus, while the example and message of Ann Lee was a necessary factor in the development of gender-inclusive God imagery, the decline in her status did not take away from this doctrine once it was firmly established.

But the establishment of gender-inclusive imagery for God never did alter certain significant elements of Shaker social structure. Women and men remained restricted to their traditional work roles. Women continued to be identified with the more internal and physically constrained domestic world, and men with the more expansive world of agriculture, construction, and business. Not until there had been a sharp decline in the number of male members were women allowed to assume the important responsibilities of the trustee position. Finally, celibacy remained a pivotal Shaker element. The acceptance of a feminine element in God did not diminish their elevation of spirit over body, nor allow them to celebrate the human capacity for sexual enjoyment and physical generativity.

Indeed, it may have been their attitudes to marriage, procreation, and community which made the appropriation of female God imagery difficult for the Shakers. For the Shakers, the Mother image was especially problematic. Against the surrounding culture's values, the good woman for the Shakers was not necessarily the woman who desired, gave birth to, and personally nurtured her children. In fact, it was considered far superior for a woman to avoid this fleshly activity altogether. For those who were already mothers, the good woman and mother was the one who gave up her children to the care of the Shaker community, who let go her close attachments, who turned her attention to her own spiritual growth and the welfare of the community as a whole.[1]

Ann Lee was the good woman and Mother of the Shakers, but not because she physically gave birth to four children. Nor was she revered because of any distinctively maternal suffering she might have experienced when she lost them. Had the Shakers not been so ambivalent over human sexuality, the idea of the mother who suffers over losing her children could have been a very productive theological route to pursue (such as, the divine Mother suffering over the loss of human souls, or—if they had had a theology of the cross—the divine Mother suffering over the salvifically necessary death of the divine Child). Instead, Ann Lee was the good mother because she turned her energies away from the physical and toward the spiritual.

A Shaker woman could not image God as Mother through personally being a mother. Nor could Shakers image God as Mother through the model of their own mothers—neither love nor glorification of one's own mother could be turned into material for the image of God. Both male and female Shakers were most highly praised when they put their loyalty to the group above their attachment to their biological mothers and fathers. Yet, in spite of this evacuation of the content of the Mother image, the Shakers could think of no better female image for God than Mother. The female Shakers thus had the ambiguous and difficult role of being, at best, symbolic mothers—while eschewing the physiological and natural-affectional components. And all Shakers had the difficult task of relating to God as Mother without the possibility of using their own mothers as prototypes, paradigms, or exemplars. Because of the deep traditional roots of the Father God model and its societal reinforcements, the consequences of the Shaker rejection of this biological parental role were not as adverse for the paternal image of God.

It is likely that the Shakers' particular ambivalence over the biological mother role was one reason it was so difficult, especially at the outset, for this new image of God as Mother to seize the imagination of average Shaker believers and affect their experience of God. Even when the wisdom aspect was stressed in the Shaker image of Holy Mother Wisdom, many believers in their testimonies did not demonstrate particular attraction to this female image of God. Thus the Shaker theologians were successful in developing a female image of God, and the leadership in schooling members in it, but this theological image does not appear to have greatly affected the way members experienced God, at least in the decades immediately following the formalization of this theological theme.

Implications for the Contemporary Discussion

In the contemporary church, an understanding of the inadequacy of male imagery for God is emerging. Among some people a tentative consensus holds that it is both legitimate and necessary to expand imagery for God. While this work ought to continue, the Shaker example cautions against too heavy a reliance on the pragmatic component in the argumentation for gender-inclusive God imagery. That is, the Shaker example does not support the assumption that changes in imagery and doctrine will be self-reinforcing and productive of personal and structural changes once the new theology is formulated. Rather, the Shaker case suggests that formalized changes in religious imagery are not adequate alone to powerfully and directly shape changes in experience. Imagery must emerge from, confirm, and relate to changes in experience, and be encouraged and reinforced by changes in social structure.

Furthermore, the Shaker experience also suggests that, even when coupled with other reinforcing elements—such as social structure and liturgical expression, as was certainly the case for the Shakers—formal changes in a group's teachings cannot be expected to have quick, dramatic, or even predictable effect. The efforts of church leaders to formulate a coherent gender-inclusive doctrine of God may eventually have an effect, but the ways in which it will interact with religious experience cannot be predicted, even when it is carefully taught and ritualized.

To be credible, efficacious, and persuasive—indeed to be an authentic and reliable interpretation of the faith of the group—adjustments to doctrine must emerge from the group's religious experience as a whole, even though leaders take on the task of systematizing and formulating it theologically. Without this "consensus fidelium" it is unlikely that the constructive work of theology will move beyond the theoretical stage. Although theology has a heuristic task (that is, to guide the church toward new theological insights) as well as the task of expressing and formalizing the experience of the faithful, these two roles must be performed concurrently.

In fact, even the leadership may need further experiential confirmation of insights that arise from careful theological reflection. For example, in the Shaker case it is significant that, even after formulating one of the foundational statements of gender-inclusive God imagery, elder and writer Calvin Green needed a separate experiential awakening to the power of female imagery before he agreed to help edit Paulina Bates' book of messages from Holy Mother Wisdom. All of this makes more graphic the dynamic interplay between imagery, doctrine, and experience.

Another critical factor from the Shaker experience that can be related to contemporary theology is the connection between the Shaker dual christology and their God imagery. A cursory review of Shaker theology might lead to the impression that Shaker experience demonstrates that a gender-dual christological approach to the core symbolism of Christianity is essential to gender-inclusive imagery for God. But a closer reading of the history of Shaker theology does not confirm this impression. For gender-inclusive God imagery was eventually detached from the dual christology that had only been important to the Shaker belief structure for a part of their history.

The real contribution of the Shaker experience is its demonstration of the power in the Christ-come-in-community message that Ann Lee proclaimed and that later believers returned to. The compelling example of Ann Lee, her message that Christ could come to each believer, and her charismatic creation of community, may well have been an adequate impetus to the eventual insight that God encompassed both male and female—without the need for a dual christology. Rather than demonstrating the need to elevate certain individuals to christological status, the Shakers teach that it is more empowering to understand the spirit of Christ as accessible to each human being and to live in the power of that belief. Additionally, since their entire structure was built upon the divine message they believed Ann Lee had brought to them, a neo-pragmatic sort of explanation for their gender-inclusive God or Christ imagery would have been totally alien to the Shaker mind.

The Shaker example also suggests that people must accept the reality of God's empowerment of actual females before being able to recognize divine gender inclusivity. And these female examples of divine empowerment and spiritual vitality must be recognized and honored as such by the entire community. Shaker history suggests that the leadership, intentions, and model of the charismatic Ann Lee were not enough. If females had not been given the opportunity to emulate Lee in leadership and service, it is unlikely that the community would have been as successful at incorporating female images into their doctrine of God and liturgical expression.

The contemporary church situation has some similarities. Here, too, women's experience and leadership have preceded theological work on God imagery. The issue of the ordination of women arose before the call for gender-inclusive God imagery. Women's increasing visibility as ordained ministers (at least in the Protestant denominations) has given impetus to the necessity to confront exclusively male God language and imagery. And the reality that women in general are using their gifts and abilities in the more visible public realm increases the dissonance experienced when the power and character of God is described solely through male images. Thus the pragmatic and apologetic arguments for changing God imagery have emerged only after significant changes were effected in the context of contemporary church and society.

The Shaker experiment also indicates that community reinforcement of gender-inclusive imagery is more decisive in achieving its usage than a reliance on gender affinity. Indeed, Shaker experience suggests that female imagery for God is not necessarily more attractive to or empowering for women than for men,[2] even though the contemporary argument from experience often presupposes this. The contemporary church would be amiss if it assumed and acted as though the creation and appropriation of female imagery for God were primarily women's work. The Shaker

157

example demonstrates that males as well as females can develop and appropriate this imagery—and that both must be equally careful not to fall back into gender stereotypes when doing so. In addition, perhaps the most important thing the Shaker teach is how difficult it is to incorporate gender into our understanding of God without reifying the traditional cultural stereotypes of male and female. The Shaker example suggests that it is at this point that the contemporary argument from experience will most readily encounter difficulty.

A study of the Shakers addresses another assumption of much of the contemporary argumentation for gender-inclusive God imagery, that is, that there is a positive correlation between gender-inclusive imagery for God and a fully egalitarian social structure. The Shaker experience shows, rather, that if such a correlation is to occur, it must be purposeful and each element must be given specific, individual attention. If an intentional community such as the Shakers—where theory and practice were so inextricably linked—did not adequately pursue this connection, great effort is even more necessary for those whose religious and everyday perspectives are much less closely intertwined.

For the Shakers, the fact that they did not fully develop the potential in this connection has more to do with the way they imaged God, than in any lack of mutually reinforcing links between God imagery and social structure. Despite Shaker claims to have freed women from the world's constraints, the gender imagery they developed conformed to traditional cultural gender patterns as much as it challenged them.

A similar dilemma may be preventing the contemporary church from successfully introducing female imagery for God. Although the Mother image appears to be a logical place to begin imaging God in female terms, this image is caught today in a crisis of meaning. Feminism has rightly spent the last two decades demonstrating (among other things) that the symbolic picture of mother, except for the most basic of physiological connections, is not culture-free at all. The cultural connotations of the mother symbol—and our particular indecisiveness today over those meanings—is one reason why this image has not found a home in the contemporary church.

In spite of a persistent, and often sensitive effort to introduce this image in the church, many ministers and seminarians report a spontaneous and often virulently negative reaction when they attempt to use maternal imagery for God. Undoubtedly this reaction reflects, in large part, our inherited misogynism. Yet the spontaneous negative reaction of the God as Mother image by many also goes beyond this. Current society is experiencing—as did the Shakers—serious confusion over the image of mother. For different, although related, reasons, neither the Shakers nor current society has a clear image of mother upon which to draw when proposing maternal imagery for God.

The contemporary ambiguity over the mother symbol has a different source from the Shaker problem, though in a way they are related. As contemporary American feminism has successfully made society aware of the cultural devaluation of and constraints put upon women as mothers, women have slowly been persuaded to pursue self-development, self-knowledge, and service to the wider world, rather than narrowly confining their efforts to the familial realm. In addition, socioeconomic factors are requiring many more mothers to work for wages, a process which predates the current feminist movement. While this situation has only recently gripped the middle class—with women again entering the work force after a period of post–World War II domestic retreat—poorer women have long had to face this tension.

Thus women as mothers today are caught in a wrenching conflict, for they must balance conflicting demands. On one side, there is the model of motherly nurture, self-sacrifice, and intimate personal attention to offspring. But this picture is in practical tension with the emerging model of self-development and responsibility to the wider world—and, for many, the demands of sheer economic survival. The serious emotional and practical tensions caused by these conflicting demands will not be resolved quickly.

Thus, when the image of God as Mother is introduced in, for example, a contemporary worship service, a serious antinomy can be created in the minds of worshipers. Emphasizing the traditional characteristics associated with motherhood, such as nurture, intimate care, and family-directed service, can create a profound sense of confusion and cognitive dissonance for many. And even if these traditional characteristics are deliberately minimized when the mother image is used, in the minds of worshipers the current confusion over the mother role is still unavoidably attached to that model.

In society today, it is not clear just who is the "good mother." Given this uncertainty, the image of God as Mother cannot help but attract a similar disharmony or ambiguity as it likely did for many Shakers. Recognizing this dilemma is not to downplay the importance and potential in the image of God as Mother, or to argue for a discontinuance of its use. Rather, it is an attempt to explain at least part of the strong reaction against this image in many contemporary churches. Much more work will have to be done on the socioeconomic and psychological levels to make the role of mother a positive and less ambiguous one, before the image of God as Mother finds a ready welcome in the church. Therefore, even if it can be demonstrated that changes in God imagery—particularly if given enough time—will eventually affect believers' religious experience (and self-consciousness and social structure), the choice of imagery must nevertheless be done with acute attention to the changing needs, experience, and understandings of the community.

Gender-Inclusive Imagery for God

Conclusions from the Shaker Study

In several important ways, Shaker God imagery actually prevented believers from fully appropriating the potential in divine gender inclusivity. Shaker imagery for God, though gender-inclusive, was not as revolutionary as some contemporary observers have assumed. The type of gender-inclusive imagery that the Shakers chose was in large part responsible for keeping believers rooted in traditional gender hierarchy. In fact, many believers' testimonies were in accord with the Society's theological formulations, even though testifiers did not go so far as to make extensive use of female imagery for God. Testifiers' adherence to the primacy of the masculine aspect of God, and to certain traditional gender stereotypes, was in keeping with the theological formulations developed by Shaker writers.

But two key factors—factors that influenced the type of gender inclusivity used by the Shaker writers in developing their doctrine of God—must be examined to determine the part they played in the inadequacy of the Shakers' formulation. The first factor was the strong reaction against the traditional trinitarian understanding of God because the Shakers were convinced it was essentially tritheistic. A second, and related, factor was the rejection of the exclusively male titles traditionally used for the three divine persons. Because, to their mind, all of reality was two-gendered, and because God created humankind in the divine image, it stood to reason that God, too, was somehow dual, encompassing both genders.

In the most formative statement of their doctrine of God, *Testimony of Christ's Second Appearing*, God was presented as essentially greater than gender, and so the divine twoness was explained first in a trans-gendered way. Thus God was essentially Supreme Intelligence, composed of the co-operating elements of Power and Wisdom. But the primary way humans could know God was through the self-manifestation of the divine twoness through the basic and obvious categories of male and female. Therefore, the two elements, Power and Wisdom, occupied the "thrones" of the Eternal Father and Holy Mother. It was through these two parental images that humankind could learn to know God. Youngs tried to avoid a simply modalistic under-standing of these two roles. Therefore, he stressed that the twoness was somehow in the substance of God—it was essential to God, not just a two-part manifestation of God's oneness done for a specific purpose and time (that is, a modalistic and/or economic view).

Whether other writers followed the more sophisticated reasoning of *Testimony of Christ's Second Appearing* is doubtful. Although Calvin Green and Seth Wells' book approached it, later writers reduced this schema to more simple components. Thus, either God was understood as essentially two gendered, or the two roles simply became modes of the one God. But it was Youngs', and especially Green and Wells', insistence on the source role of the male element, and the need for order within the Godhead, which led later writers naturally into this modalism and an increased hierarchy where the male element, as source, had primacy.

Even though the Shaker doctrine of God brought the

female element into the Godhead itself, a higher authority was nevertheless accorded the male divine element. Through the successive writings of *Testimony of Christ's Second Appearing,* the female element in Deity was conceived either as the spirit of the male side of God or as an eternal helpmate with him. Both views led to the ultimate subordination of the female to the male principle. Even though Youngs was able to keep gender out of the substantial side of God, one could nevertheless trace out a subordinationist view of gender. This was a binitarian doctrine of God, composed of the Holy Spirit (Holy Mother Wisdom) and God the Father. In line with traditional Christian two-elements efforts to introduce gender into the Trinity, the Holy Spirit as the feminine or female element was in effect subordinated to the masculine Father element in the Shaker dual God.

Thus Paulina Bates' subordination of Holy Mother Wisdom to the Eternal Father, and female to male, was congruent with formative Shaker theology. Although she gave a redemptive twist to the imagery, thereby insuring enough authority for her authorship to make her book acceptable to the leadership, her copious use of female imagery did not improve the status of the female element in God.

Likewise, the subordinationist view of gender reflected in the revival period and in individual testimonies has a clear lineage in the earlier works of theology. In spite of the strong female influence in the revival manifestations and the importance of Holy Mother Wisdom's visitations, the female element was still subsidiary to the sourceness or originary role of the male element in God. Holy Mother Wisdom was an emissary and messenger, whose authority was ultimately derived from the Eternal Father. In conclusion, the inadequacy in the Shakers' own concept of gender inclusivity to some extent prevented a full realization of their vaunted elevation of women in their society. In addition, its inadequacy may have also short-circuited the concept's potential for affecting Shaker religious experience.

Implications for the Contemporary Discussion

There are at least three major options open for those who take a gender-inclusive approach to God imagery.[3] Contemporary theology can learn from the theological choices the Shakers made, since it is faced with similar options today. The Shakers did not consciously choose one option over another—in fact, they experimented with several approaches—but the results of the decisions they made are instructive for current theological work. It is useful to briefly lay out the three main alternatives for gender-inclusive God imagery, in order to locate the Shaker usage and explore its advantages and limitations.

The first major approach to incorporating gender inclusivity into the doctrine of God assigns stereotypical feminine or female traits to a God still essentially imaged as male or masculine, so that God becomes the motherly Father.[4] This approach functions to expand the range of attributes associated with a male God symbol, and thus widens the acceptable range of behavior for men. It does not offer alternatives to women, for its effect is to incorporate aspects of the feminine stereotype into the still-dominant male image. Neither the Shakers nor contemporary feminists choose the first way, sensing its inherent limitations. Still, it is sometimes chosen by contemporary theologians who seek to address the current critique of male God imagery. But, as Elizabeth Johnson says,

> Real women are then seen as capable of representing only the feminine element of what is still the male-centered symbol of God, the fullness of which can thereby be represented only by a male person. The female can never appear as icon of God in all

divine fullness equivalent to the male. Inequality is not redressed but subtly furthered, as the androcentric structure of anthropology and the image of God remains in place and is made more appealing through the subordinate inclusion of feminine traits.[5]

The second major alternative comes closer to being truly gender inclusive. In this model, gender is taken with utmost seriousness and seen as having primal force. Gender inclusivity becomes a viable aspect of God imagery, such that God is composed of masculine and feminine elements. Building on cultural paradigms, the masculine aspect of God appropriates such attributes as power, justice, and righteousness, while the feminine aspect represents such attributes as nurture, wisdom, and life-giving. This option was explored by the Shakers and also can be attractive to many contemporary theorists. This approach may appeal especially to those who, like the Shakers, reject the traditional trinitarian understanding of God as male-oriented. But it also can be accomplished in a trinitarian framework, traditionally by having the Holy Spirit serve as the feminine element.[6]

The advantage of this alternative is that it raises femaleness into the Godhead itself, giving it ontological status. The two-elements approach to God imagery proposes to put the masculine and feminine elements of God on equal, parallel footing. As the Shakers realized, this two-element approach seems a logical, natural way to describe God, since it can be patterned on the fact of two human genders.

This method also stresses the need for revaluing and elevating that cluster of attributes identified as feminine. In the current discussion, concern is sometimes expressed that when a distinctively female way of being human is not preserved, and androgyny is proposed instead, male patterns, in effect, are declared ultimate, and female ways of being are denied. Whether these male and female ways are seen as biological[7] or sociological, the concern is to reverse the destructive hegemony of such male-associated attributes as competitiveness, desire to dominate, extreme individualism, and the glorification of physical force. Instead, such female-associated attributes as interrelatedness, nurture, mutual support, and the primacy of relationship are expected to prosper on the worldly plane when given an ontological place in the nature of God.

This argument has a certain persuasiveness, certainly from the pragmatic and apologetic points of view, since it capitalizes on existing cultural patterns. In addition, it makes clear an essential truth for our day. That is, for the sake of our world we must elevate and promote those characteristics associated with femaleness. Yet the Shaker example demonstrates some inherent limitations in the two-elements method of doing this. The practical disadvantage is that the decision about what is masculine and feminine often is based on little more than cultural stereotypes. When current theology, using the argument from experience for gender-inclusive God imagery, posits that we will learn about feminine or female imagery for God largely through the experience of women, it risks limiting itself to existing forms of gender, rather than enlarging our range of possibilities for being truly human.

The Shakers, in taking experience as source and norm in order to transcend cultural restrictions, ended up accepting many of these limitations. Even though they avoided the complications and restrictions of traditional family life through their celibacy, they could think of few female images for God beyond mother. And when they tried to assert God's unity, they fell into the trap of finding that unity in the masculine element. Each of the two reasons they gave for this drew heavily upon traditional mainstream ideas of gender, arguing that the masculine element is the source of the feminine, and that one final authority is needed—that is the male.

That the Shakers chose to consider the masculine and feminine elements of God in a binitarian rather than a trinitarian form—thus presumably putting these elements on parallel, equal footing—did not serve to end the subordination of the feminine element, nor prevent the reification of cultural stereotypes. In effect, theirs was a binitarian God composed of Father and Spirit (Holy Mother Wisdom), with Father in the traditional role of source and authority. The Christ Spirit was subsidiary to both elements in the Godhead, yet even on this level, Jesus' embodiment of the Christ Spirit was often given a higher status than Ann Lee's manifestation of it.

Because of the current sensitivity to the dynamics of male dominance, it is easier today to avoid the ensnarement of positing the male as source and authority, either in a two-element or a trinitarian doctrine of God. But it is not clear that proposing the female aspect of God as the new source—as source of both inner-divine unity, and of the world (with creation now imaged as birthing)—would be a significant improvement. Understanding a Mother God as source of inner-divine unity could still be used to produce a modalistic or hierarchical view of gender since it simply reverses the gender associated with these functions.

Understanding God as source of the world—the way a mother is source of a child—is more biologically natural and experientially based, but it does not do away with the negative potential in the reification of gender stereotypes, since it still links women primarily with biological function. In addition, the traditional core divine attribute of aseity, or absolute independence, would have to be reconceived under this new paradigm since giving birth has more necessity attached to it than does creating. This could be a profitable endeavor, since God's absolute independence has been used to buttress a primary characteristic of the male stereotype, nonrelational individualism. Alternatively, perhaps the focus on source, so long dominant in western trinitarian thought, will have to be the element reconsidered by contemporary theology and another way found to explain the unity of the Godhead and the God/world relationship.

Nevertheless, the male-and-female-dimensions approach to God does not avoid problems—it creates different ones. By reifying gender, we actually limit the available fund of imagery for God. We restrict ourselves to existing patterns, and tie our understanding of gender to largely cultural paradigms that developed for various contextual reasons, many of them no longer suitable. And in a two-element description of the inner relationships in God, we either reify the stereotypes (even though we now work to value them equally), or promote a modalistic and/or hierarchical understanding of gender in God.

The third approach to gender-inclusive imagery is the most difficult to achieve since it neither draws upon a major stream of interpretation in the Christian tradition nor fits into existing gender stereotypes as the previous two approaches readily do. In spite of these limitations, it is congruent with the "grammar" of the Christian faith and has the potential to avoid the reification of gender, with its attendant problems. This approach images God as both male and female. However, it does not do this because of any value the images may have in providing information about gender. Rather, as Suzanne Johnson says, for this approach the main benefit of gender-inclusive imagery becomes its ability to point to the incomprehensibility of God. The Shakers moved toward this view by positing God as essentially Supreme Intelligence, with a dual character that essentially was not gendered, but encompassed gender and communicated to humans in familiar gendered forms. However, because of the Shakers' virulent rejection of the Trinity, and their strong reliance on natural and experiential sources for their theology, they ultimately were restricted by their binitarian view to a masculine-and-feminine-dimensions approach to God.

The Potential in a Trinitarian Conception

Contemporary theology has much work to do to successfully incorporate the fact, and symbolic potential, of our two-gendered human condition into an understanding of God. It must decide how the reality of two genders can be valued, how this unity-in-diversity pattern of humankind can be perceived as enriching, without reifying gender and thus restricting our image of God (and ourselves) to existing patterns. A revitalized trinitarian doctrine of God has the potential to do this. In fact, as early as the medieval period, Richard of St. Victor (d. 1173) showed aptly why divine love as community is not well imaged by a two-personed symbol, but is best communicated through a threeness. Though he did not consider gender, his work does suggest the excellence and attractiveness of a divine plurality symbolized by three, rather than by two.[8]

It must be asserted at the outset that the traditional trinitarian doctrine of God, with its masculine terminology, has been used by many to justify the subordination of women. Yet such a use of the Trinity is not essential to its functioning as a basic unit in the "grammar" of the Christian faith. Rather, certain integral aspects of the traditional view—especially its dynamic of mutual equality, interpenetration *(perichoresis),* harmony, and dynamic cooperation within the Godhead—hold promise for contemporary theology as it wrestles with the gender issue.

This constructive approach to Trinity images God as a coequal, interconnected community of divine persons, operating in a completely harmonious and mutually loving manner. Freely and out of this abundance, the divine love spills over to create, and then to intimately love, that creation. Such a trinitarian community avoids the gender dualism endemic to the two-elements approach. The process it suggests can also be productively used in describing and providing a model for human relationships. On both the divine and the creation levels, this trinitarian interpersonal understanding can incorporate gender without overstressing it in the way the two-elements approach tends to do. With its roots in the social analogy of the Trinity, such a reconceived trinitarian view has more room to contain gender—without reifying it—than a binitarian conception. The inner-relationship within the divine plurality can then be analogized on the model of a community of persons, and instead of stressing the personality of God, the church can consider personality *in* God.

This is not to advocate some random intermixing of human characteristics in an effort to transcend gender. This is neither possible nor desirable, for it is true that a typically androgynous approach to gender encourages the dominant, male-related attributes to prevail. But to seek a solution to male dominance by rooting gender stereotypes in God only causes a further hardening of them—as the Shakers demonstrate—and does not resolve many of the intractable problems we now seek to redress.

It is not simply a matter of adding a female element to the traditional trinitarian conception of God, as some attempts to use the masculine-and-feminine-dimension approach to gender inclusivity have done. This traditional approach of making the Holy Spirit the feminine dimension has had only limited and qualified results.[9] Even so, some modern theologians have carried on this tradition, in an effort to preserve the traditional male trinitarian terms of Father and Son, while at the same time accommodating a female element.[10]

In this approach, the Holy Spirit—which always has played a more amorphous role in Western theology—is designated the female element, sometimes even being referred to as she. In spite of initial appearances, this approach actually does not challenge the dominant male image of God. Not only is the female element numerically in the minority, but, more importantly, the female aspect assumes a secondary, even though integral, role. As Elizabeth Johnson says,

> The overarching framework . . . remains androcentric, with the male principle still dominant and sovereign. The Spirit even as God remains the 'third' person, easily subordinated to the other two, since she proceeds from them and is sent by them to mediate their presence and bring to completion what they have initiated.[11]

Although this is not the binitarian God of the Shakers, it is nevertheless a two-elements approach. While it maintains a sort of superficial continuity with the tradition, the approach actually works against the essence of a trinitarian understanding of God since the female image is restricted to one aspect of the triune God, and the least well-defined aspect, at that. True mutual harmony, coequality and perichoresis are made difficult when each divine person is linked inextricably to a particular gender. This approach does not answer the modern critique of male God imagery.

Another way must be found to incorporate female imagery into the potentially rich dynamic of a trinitarian understanding of God.[12] In this effort certain essential elements need to be included in order to avoid past problems. First, images must be drawn from both male and

171

female personhood. But these images cannot be divided into sets of attributes or clusters of stereotypes. Instead, male and female images must each be both holistic and equivalent. Although non-personal and non-gender-specific images also can be used, it is desirable to preserve the language of person since this "evokes in a unique way the mysteriousness, nonmanipulability, and freedom of action associated with God."[13]

Second, care must be taken to draw images from a wide variety of social classes, ethnic and racial groups, and differing life experiences. In this respect, those who use the argument from experience when explaining how images change, make a crucial contribution. Images are most powerful and most attractive when they arise from, and speak to, experience. Even though images can be used heuristically—that is, to provoke new connections and thus facilitate new behavior—they must at the same time connect to lived experience.

Third, an effort must be made not only to derive images from contemporary experience, but also to provide linkages to those images presented in Scripture and Christian tradition. A religion which fails to maintain contact with its past demonstrates not only hubris, but an impoverishment of its collective memory and message. And, as some scholars have shown, there is untapped potential in many of the traditional sources when examined through the new lens of a gender-inclusive hermeneutic.[14]

Fourth, and most important, this approach must enhance our appreciation of God's essential incomprehensibility. Any new method to incorporate female imagery into the Trinity must lead to the realization that God is not depicted adequately by either male or female images—or even by both together. Ultimately, we must admit our inability to encapsulate and limit God.

Although these are only preliminary suggestions toward

such an effort, the expectation is that through such a reconceived trinitarian, gender-inclusive understanding of God, the idolatry of one-gendered imagery for God will be broken. The Shaker example shows that trying to subvert this idolatry through the reification of gender does not have the same potential to do this exceedingly difficult task.

The Shakers have provided invaluable assistance. They have demonstrated the theological and practical problems in a two-elements approach to gender-inclusive imagery for God. Their example has warned against expecting too much from the changing of imagery. And they have shown the difficulty in predicting or controlling individual believers' use of imagery. Nevertheless, the Shaker example teaches us that gender-inclusive imagery for God has the power and the potential to break the hold of gender hierarchy. This can only happen under certain conditions. To affect change, gender-inclusive imagery must emerge from and be validated by experience. It must be theologically formulated with great care. And, finally, gender-inclusive imagery must be reinforced by a social structure that values the contributions and characteristics of *all* its members.

NOTES

1. Gender Imagery for God: The Complexity of the Issue

1. One of the earliest articulations in the contemporary movement of the critique of male imagery for God, and certainly the most influential for American feminism, was Mary Daly's *Beyond God the Father: Toward a Philosophy of Women's Liberation* (Boston: Beacon, 1973).

2. See, e.g., Mary Daly, *Gyn/Ecology: The Metaethics of Radical Feminism* (Boston: Beacon, 1978). The literature on this subject is abundant. In addition to Daly's numerous works, some additional examples include: *Womanspirit Rising: A Feminist Reader in Religion*, ed. Carol P. Christ and Judith Plaskow (New York: Harper & Row, 1979); *Beyond Androcentrism: New Essays on Women and Religion*, ed. Rita Gross (Missoula, Mont.: Scholars Press, 1977); Sallie McFague, *Models of God: Theology for an Ecological, Nuclear Age* (Philadelphia: Fortress, 1987); Rosemary Ruether, *Sexism and God-Talk: Toward a Feminist Theology* (Boston: Beacon, 1983); Diane Tennis, *Is God the Only Reliable Father* (Philadelphia: Westminster, 1985); Anne E. Carr, *Transforming Grace: Christian Tradition and Women's Experience* (San Francisco: Harper & Row, 1988).

3. McFague, *Models of God*, p. xiv. See this and her previous book, *Metaphorical Theology: Models of God in Religious Language* (Philadelphia: Fortress, 1982), for a detailed discussion of model, metaphor, and concept, as well as comments about the feminist critique of language.

4. Barbara Starrett, "The Metaphors of Power," in *The Politics of Women's Spirituality: Essays in the Rise of Spiritual Power Within the Feminist Movement*, ed. Charlene Spretnak (Garden City, N.Y.: Doubleday, 1982), p. 186.

5. Sandra M. Schneiders, "The Effects of Women's Experience on Their Spirituality," in *Spirituality Today*, Vol. 35, no. 2 (Summer 1983): 102.

6. Naomi R. Goldenberg, *The Changing of the Gods: Feminism and the End of Traditional Religions* (Boston: Beacon, 1979), p. 82.

7. Joan Chamberlain Engelsman, *The Feminine Dimension of the Divine* (Philadelphia: Westminster, 1979), p. 156.

8. Although McFague deals with considerably more than female imagery for God, her work in *Models of God* supports this argument.

9. Rosemary Radford Ruether, "Motherearth and the Megamachine: A Theology of Liberation in a Feminine, Somatic and Ecological Perspective," in *Womanspirit Rising*, ed. Christ and Plaskow, pp. 51-52.

10. See, e.g., *Embodied Love: Sensuality and Relationship as Feminist Values*, ed. Paula M. Cooey, Sharon A. Farmer, and Mary Ellen Ross (San Francisco: Harper & Row, 1987).

11. Two of the earliest books from this "second wave" are Betty Friedan, *The Feminine Mystique* (New York: Dell Publishing Co., 1963), and Simone De Beauvoir, *The Second Sex*, trans. and ed. H. M. Parshley (New York: Vintage,

1974). Both of these works treat the problem of gender stereotyping in work roles.

12. McFague, *Models of God*, pp. 37, xi, xiii, and passim.

13. Gordon D. Kaufman, *The Theological Imagination: Constructing the Concept of God* (Philadelphia: Westminster, 1981).

14. This is what William Hamilton predicts will come of the feminist effort to develop the Goddess image. See, e.g., Lloyd Steffan, "The Dangerous God: A Profile of William Hamilton," *The Christian Century* (Sept. 27, 1989): 844-47.

15. Sheila Greene Davaney, "The Limits of the Appeal to Women's Experience," in *Shaping New Vision: Gender and Values in American Culture*, ed. Clarissa W. Atkinson, Constance H. Buchanan and Margaret R. Miles (Ann Arbor: U.M.I. Research Press, 1987), p. 48.

16. Elizabeth A. Johnson, C.S.J., "The Incomprehensibility of God and the Image of God Male and Female," in *Theological Studies*, 45:3 (Sept. 1984): 445.

17. For a schema of views on the theological relationship of Christ and culture, see H. Richard Niebuhr, *Christ and Culture* (New York: Harper & Row, 1951).

18. Engelsman, *The Feminine Dimension of the Divine*, p. 156.

19. Ruether, *Sexism and God-Talk*, p. 46.

20. Carol P. Christ, "Embodied Thinking: Reflections on Feminist Theological Method," in *Journal of Feminist Studies in Religion*, vol. 5:1 (Spring 1989): 14. See this article for an effort, against neo-pragmatism, to root new imagery in truth-claims.

21. Phyllis Trible, *God and the Rhetoric of Sexuality* (Philadelphia: Fortress, 1978), especially her discussion of Gen. 1:27.

22. For a discussion of this, see Johnson, "The Incomprehensibility of God and the Image of God Male and Female."

23. Sandra M. Schneiders, *Women and the Word: The Gender of God in the New Testament and the Spirituality of Women* (New York: Paulist, 1986), pp. 9-10, 19.

24. Ruether, *Sexism and God-Talk*, p. 71. See also Elisabeth Schüssler Fiorenza, *In Memory of Her: A Feminist Reconstruction of Christian Origins* (New York: Crossroad, 1983). For a critical perspective on the appeal to women's experience see Sheila Greene Davaney, "Problems with Feminist Theory: Historicity and the Search for Sure Foundations," in *Embodied Love*, ed. Cooey, Farmer, and Ross, pp. 79-95; and idem, "The Limits of the Appeal to Women's Experience," in *Shaping New Vision: Gender and Values in American Culture*, ed. Clarissa W. Atkinson, Constance H. Buchanan, and Margaret R. Miles (Ann Arbor: U.M.I. Research Press, 1987), pp. 31-49.

25. I first heard the phrase "the God who loves women" in 1979 from Barbara Waugh, then co-director of the Center for Women and Religion at the Graduate Theological Union, Berkeley, Calif., when I was serving on the staff there. Whether or not it originated with her, I am indebted to her for this evocative image.

26. George A. Lindbeck, *The Nature of Doctrine: Religion and Theology in a Postliberal Age* (Philadelphia: Westminster, 1984).

27. Ibid., pp. 33-34.

28. McFague, *Models of God*, p. 19. She and Gordon Kaufman have debated this point, since he holds that personal terms are not especially useful or relevant. See, e.g., Gordon Kaufman, "Models of God: Is Metaphor Enough?" in *Religion and Intellectual Life*, 5 (Spring 1988): 11-18. See also Kaufman, *Theology for a Nuclear Age* (Philadelphia: Westminster, 1985).

29. E.g., *Embodied Love,* ed. Cooey, Farmer, and Ross.

30. This represents the classic statement of this position. Carol Christ, "Why Women Need the Goddess: Phenomenological, Psychological, and Political Reflections," passim, *Womanspirit Rising,* ed. Christ and Plaskow. See also Mary Daly's numerous works.

31. See, e.g., Virginia Ramey Mollenkott, *The Divine Feminine: The Biblical Imagery of God as Female* (New York: Crossroad, 1981); and Leonard Swidler, *Biblical Affirmations of Women* (Philadelphia: Westminster, 1979).

32. McFague, *Models of God,* p. 100.

33. The basis for this schema is presented in Johnson, in her article "The Incomprehensibility of God and the Image of God Male and Female," although Shaker theology adds a significant variation to it, as will be demonstrated in chapter 3.

34. See Johnson, "The Incomprehensibility of God and the Image of God Male and Female," as well as chapter 5, for additional information on this.

35. See, e.g., Susan Setta, "Women of the Apocalypse: The Reincorporation of the Feminine through the Second Coming of Christ in Ann Lee" (unpublished dissertation, Pennsylvania State University, 1979). For a discussion of those who see feminist inclinations in the Shakers, see Marjorie Procter-Smith, *Women in Shaker Community and Worship: A Feminist Analysis of the Uses of Religious Symbolism* (Lewiston/Queenston: The Edwin Mellen Press, 1985), introduction and passim. One recent commentator understands a proto-feminism in their doctrine of celibacy; see Sally L. Kitch, *Chaste Liberation: Celibacy and Female Cultural Status* (Champaign: University of Illinois, 1989).

36. Ruether, *Sexism and God-Talk,* pp. 21-22; 99-100.

37. Among others who agree with this point are Procter-Smith, *Women in Shaker Community and Worship.*

2. The Development of the Shaker Idea of God

1. Both Procter-Smith, *Women in Shaker Community and Worship: A Feminist Analysis of the Uses of Religious Symbolism* (Lewiston/Queenston: The Edwin Mellon Press, 1985) and Robley Whitson, *The Shakers: Two Centuries of Spiritual Reflection* (New York: Paulist, 1983) agree that the idea of divine gender inclusivity likely was not present at the outset of Shaker teaching. Some scholars, however, still assert that Ann Lee taught a gender-inclusive God. The most influential and possibly earliest contemporary proponent of this view is Edward Deming Andrews, *The People Called Shakers* (New York: Dover, 1963). He may have gotten this idea from the writings of certain late nineteenth- and early twentieth-century Shaker writers, such as Frederick Evans.

2. Many histories of the Shakers (although not those by the Shakers) claim them as ex-Quakers, but this has been disputed. See, e.g., Clarke Garrett, *Spirit Possession and Popular Religion: From the Camisards to the Shakers* (Baltimore: Johns Hopkins, 1987), p. 142.

3. Benjamin S. Youngs, *Testimony of Christ's Second Appearing,* 1st edition (Lebanon, Ohio: John MacClean, 1808), p. 23-24. Scholars dispute whether Lee actually received this vision in prison, as legend holds, or at another point. There is also disagreement over whether the group so spontaneously

recognized Lee's leadership. It is possible that a power struggle took place between Lee and the Wardleys, and Lee chose to leave England with her supporters. See, e.g., Procter-Smith, *Women in Shaker Community and Worship*, pp. 4-9; and Stephen Marini, *Radical Sects of Revolutionary New England* (Cambridge: Harvard, 1982), p. 40. Henri Desroche, *The American Shakers: From Neo-Christianity to Presocialism* (Amherst: University of Massachusetts, 1971), pp. 52f, argues there was a split.

4. "James and I lodge together; but we do not touch each other any more than two babes. You may return home and do likewise," the Wardleys told her; *Testimonies of the Life, Character, Revelations of Our Ever Blessed Mother Ann Lee, and the Elders with Her Through Whom the Word of Eternal Life was Opened in this Day of Christ's Second Appearing: Collected from Living Witnesses, By Order of the Ministry, in Union with the Church* (Hancock, Mass.: J. Tallcott and J. Deming, 1816), p. 49. This Shaker source also says that "in early youth, she had a great abhorrence of the fleshly co-habitation of the sexes; and so great was her sense of its impurity, that she often admonished her mother against it; which coming to her father's ears, he threatened and actually attempted to whip her," as quoted in Flo Morse, *The Shakers and the World's People* (Hanover: University Press of New England, 1980), p. 11. Procter-Smith, *Women in Shaker Community and Worship*, p. 7, argues that the Wardleys did not teach celibacy.

5. See Garrett, *Spirit Possession and Popular Religion*, pp. 147, 156, and passim. He disputes a standard interpretation that Lee's doctrine of celibacy was, in part, her unconscious protest against the wretched living conditions of early industrialized Manchester. Garrett says the area did not develop to that extent until the years after Lee left for America.

6. Youngs, *Testimony of Christ's Second Appearing*, 4th edition (Albany, N.Y.: The United Society, 1856), p. 619.

7. *Testimonies of the Life, Character, Revelations and Doctrines of Our Ever Blessed Mother Ann Lee* (1816), p. 49.

8. Ibid. These remembrances were likely gathered a few years previous to the publication.

9. But Youngs has her saying " 'I am *Ann* the *Word*,' " and comments, "signifying that in her dwelt the *Word*," *Testimony of Christ's Second Appearing*, 1808 ed., p. 23-24. Andrews believes she did see herself as a Christ figure. *People Called Shakers*, p. 12.

10. *Testimonies of the Life, Revelations and Doctrine of Our Ever Blessed Mother Ann Lee* (1816), see, e.g., pp. 206-11.

11. See excerpts of observers' comments in, e.g., Morse, *The Shakers and the World's People*, passim. Scholarly opinion ranges widely around how Lee saw herself. For example, Desroche sees her as a deluded person with "hypertrophy" of self-esteem who actually believed she emanated from the Godhead, *The American Shakers*, p. 54. Whitson, on the other hand, contends she simply had a powerful experience of Christ and wanted to help her followers do likewise; *The Shakers*, p. 3 and passim.

12. *Testimonies of the Life, Character, Revelations and Doctrines of Our Ever Blessed Mother Ann Lee* (1816), pp. 321-32. Procter-Smith makes the same point, *Women in Shaker Community and Worship*, pp. 20-22.

13. Ibid., p. 21. Procter-Smith also deals with the issue of the justification of Lee's leadership, but from a somewhat different perspective; *Women in Shaker Community and Worship*, pp. 14-16.

14. Andrews also suggests this development arose from practical necessity,

but adds to it the assumption that by this action the Shakers were already working from a "doctrine of a male and female messiahship." *People Called Shakers,* p. 56. I agree with Procter-Smith that "he would seem to have cause-and-effect reversed." *Women in Shaker Community and Worship,* p. vii.

15. Procter-Smith mentions five women, one of whom was Lucy Wright, an eventual leader of the Shakers, *Women in Shaker Community and Worship,* p. 17.

16. See Andrews, *People Called Shakers,* p. 21. Garrett contends, however, that "the nineteenth-century tradition that has Ann Lee naming him as the future leader is surely apocryphal," Garrett, *Spirit Possession and Popular Religion,* p. 222.

17. Calvin Green, "Biographic Memoir of the Life, Character, & Important Events, in the Ministration of Mother Lucy Wright" (Cleveland, Ohio: Western Reserve Historical Society, Shaker manuscript collection [hereafter WRHS Shaker Collection]), VI:B-27, p. 9.

18. Priscilla Brewer makes this point in *Shaker Communities, Shaker Lives* (Hanover/London: University of New England, 1986), p. 18.

19. Green, "Biographic Memoirs . . . of Mother Lucy Wright," pp. 16-17.

20. Valentine Rathbun, *Reasons Offered for Leaving the Shakers* (Pittsfield, Mass., 1800), p. 9; as cited in Brewer, *Shaker Communities, Shaker Lives,* p. 19.

21. Joseph Meacham, *A Concise Statement of the Principles of the Only True Church According to the Gospel of the Present Appearances of Christ Together with a Letter from James Whittaker to His Natural Relations in England. Dated October 8th, 1785* (Bennington, Vt.: Haswell and Russell, 1790). Given the Shaker doctrine of progressive revelation, it would not be suspect, however, for Calvin Green to later look back (since he did not write Wright's biography until 1861) and credit Meacham with the realization that there must be a mother in the Parental order and that it should be Lucy. "Biographic Memoir . . . of Mother Lucy Wright," p. 14. Brewer contends that Meacham may have been modifying his message so as not to shock the world. She also notes that in inner-Society writings, Meacham refers to Christ in female form. *Shaker Communities, Shaker Lives,* p. 25.

22. Karen Kay Nickless makes this point in her M.A. thesis, "The Origins of Shaker Feminism" (University of South Carolina, 1982), p. 17. The entire thesis sets out to prove that feminism was only imported into Shakerism toward the end of the nineteenth century and was not an original part of its proclamation or intention.

23. E.g., see Brewer, *Shaker Communities, Shaker Lives,* p. 51f.

24. Youngs, *Testimony,* 1856 ed., p. viii. See also, e.g., p. 9 in 1808 ed. where he says seekers must "free themselves of those pernicious superstitions and false doctrines of Antichrist" and that this new work "was not to be according to the systems of human invention," and p. 10 where he insists that this work "is not to be considered as any *creed* or *form of government.*"

25. George Lindbeck refers to the "inescapability of doctrine," *The Nature of Doctrine: Religion and Theology in a Postliberal Age* (Philadelphia: Westminster, 1984), p. 74.

26. Evidences can be seen in the observations of outsiders. E.g., an observer writing for the *American Magazine,* 1787, referred to a Shaker belief that the persons of the Trinity were emanations of a single divine power, and revealed other theological concepts that had been expressed to the writer. See Garrett, *Spirit Possession and Popular Religion,* pp. 216-17.

27. There is a lack of scholarly agreement here. One side, represented by Whitson (and his student John Morgan), claims that "there is no normativeness in any established form or formulation, for all such merely bear witness to the level of development . . . at that moment." Whitson, *The Shakers*, pp. 2-3. But others—such as Desroche; Stephen Marini, "New England Folk Religions 1770-1815: The Sectarian Impulse in Revolutionary Society" (Ph.D. dissertation, Harvard, 1975); and Michael Taylor, "An Ethical Analysis of Confessions, Celibacy, and Community of Interest in the Shakers from 1770 to 1905" (Ph.D. dissertation, Harvard, 1973)—would agree with Andrews that "in their doctrine is their strength." Andrews, *People Called Shakers*, p. 230. I contend that although there was no formal creed or approved corpus, a certain consistency and direction can be viewed in the history of Shaker theological writings.

28. Procter-Smith discusses the uses of these terms in chapter 1 of *Women in Shaker Community and Worship*.

29. *Testimonies Concerning the Character and Ministry of Mother Ann Lee and the First Witnesses of the Gospel of Christ's Second Appearing; Given by Some of the Aged Brethren and Sisters of the United Society, Including a Few Sketches of Their Own Religious Experience: Approved by the Church* (Albany: Packard & Van Benthuysen, 1827), pp. 12-13.

30. Ibid., p. 29.

31. Ibid., p. 30.

32. Valentine Rathbun, *Some Brief Hints of a Religious Scheme Taught and Propagated by a Number of Europeans, Living in a Place Called Nisquennia in the State of New York* (Hartford, Conn.: n.p. 1783), p. 110.

33. As quoted in John Symonds, *Thomas Brown and the Angels: A Study in Enthusiasm* (London: Hutchinson, 1961), pp. 92, 143; based on Thomas Brown, *An Account of the People Called Shakers: Their Faith, Doctrines, and Practice, Exemplified in the Life, Conversations, and Experience of the Author during the Time he Belonged to the Society, to Which is Affixed a History of Their Rise and Progress to the Present Day* (Troy, N.Y.: Parker & Bliss, 1812).

34. Although this "spirit christology" was not a full pneumatology, its emphasis on the indwelling of the Spirit of God echoes a theme that had earlier been an element in the theological milieu surrounding Shakerism. See, e.g., Goeffrey F. Nuttalls, *The Holy Spirit in Puritan Faith and Experience* (Oxford: Basil Blackwell, 1946).

35. Whitson finds two traditions in Shaker theology to explain Ann Lee. One is the "analogy-by-symmetry" school, which stressed that gender inclusivity is constitutive of all levels of reality, represented by Youngs. The other is the "union of believers" school, which stressed the community's role in embodying the Christ Spirit, represented by Dunlavy. *Shaker Theological Sources*, iii. This is also held by John Morgan, "Communitarian Communism as a Religious Experience: Exemplified in the Development of Shaker Theology" (Ph.D. dissertation, Hartford Seminary Foundation, 1972), passim. I do not find two simultaneous and distinct traditions, although I agree with Whitson that the height of reverence for Lee was during the revival period of Mother Ann's Work (see Whitson, *The Shakers*, p. 44).

36. C. E. Sears, *A Treatise on the Second Coming of Christ* (Rochester, N.Y.: Daily Democrat Steam Printing House, 1867), p. 17.

37. Geo. Albert Lomas, *Plain Talks upon Practical Religion, Being Candid Answers to Earnest Inquirers* (Albany: Van Benthuysen, 1873), p. 14.

38. See, e.g., Anna White, *The Motherhood of God* (Canaan Four Corners: Berkshire Industrial Farm Press, 1903).

39. The subsiding importance of Ann Lee can be seen, e.g., in the successive revisions of the early *Testimonies*. Thomas Swain has noted that a pattern "emerged [that] was correlated with a time factor; the further the text was away from the actual period of original experience, the more abstract the representation the person of Ann Lee became." Thomas Swain, "The Evolving Expressions of the Religious and Theological Experiences of a Community: A Comparative Study of the Shaker *Testimonies* from Oral Traditions to Written Forms as Preserved in Four Documents," *Shaker Quarterly*, 12 (Spring 1972): 3-31; (Summer 1972): 43-67, p. 48.

40. Anon., *The Story of Shakerism by One Who Knows* (East Canterbury, N.H.: Shakers, 1910), p. 9.

41. Calvin Green and Seth Youngs Wells, *Summary View of the Millennial Church, or United Society of Believers (Commonly Called Shakers) Comprising the Rise, Progress and Practical Order of the Society: Together with the General Principles of Their Faith and Testimony. Published by Order of the Ministry, in Union with the Church* (Albany: Packard and Benthuysen, 1823).

42. Isaac Reiter, ed. Carl M. Becker, "They Suffer No One to Spit on the Floor . . ." in *Communal Societies*, vol. 8 (1988): 123.

43. Catherine Allen, *The Questions of the Day* (n.p. 1888?), p. 5, published as a pamphlet, possibly first appeared in Shaker periodical.

44. Green and Wells, *Summary View of the Millennial Church*, p. xiv.

45. See, e.g., Youngs' chapter "The Holy Scriptures," *Testimony of Christ's Second Appearing*, and John Dunlavy's chapter "On the Truth of Revelation," in *The Manifesto, or a Declaration of the Doctrine and Practice of the Church of Christ* (Pleasant Hill, Ky.: The United Society, 1818).

46. Estelle B. Freedman speaks of the distinction being made in that era between the procreative and erotic elements of sexuality. She says that although the Shakers proscribed procreation "they did allow for sensual expression through ritual dances, visions, and trances." "Sexuality in Nineteenth-Century America: Behavior, Ideology, and Politics," in *Reviews in American History*, vol. 10 (1982): 203.

47. Henry M. Stone, [untitled testimony], New Lebanon, N.Y., Dec. 10, 1843 (WRHS, Shaker collection), VI:A-6. Stone wrote this at thirty-seven-years-old, having joined just two years earlier. Stone left the Society nine years later.

48. Symonds, *Thomas Brown and the Angels*, p. 132.

49. Brewer, *Shaker Communities, Shaker Lives*, p. 43.

50. Nicholas Briggs, "Forty Years a Shaker," *Granite Monthly* (Jan. 1921): 27.

51. Ibid.

52. James Whittaker, for example, is especially vehement against his natural family, as revealed in his 1785 letter to them, reprinted at the end of Meacham's *A Concise Statement*.

53. The Millennial Laws state that two or three "brethren . . . are sufficient to go to the great and wicked cities to trade for any one family," as quoted in Andrews, *People Called Shakers*, p. 258. These rules, originally verbal, became codified and written down (in various recensions) after Lucy Wright's death. Procter-Smith contends, however, that women's spiritual lives were far from restricted by the bounds of their domestic work. *Women in Shaker Community and Worship*, p. 203.

54. Frederick Marryat commented that the men looked "ruddy, strong and vigorous" and the women "so pallid, so unearthly in their complexions, that it gave you the idea that they had been taken from their coffins a few hours after their decease." *A Diary in America,* 3 vols. (London: Longmans, Orme, 1839), I:117-18; as quoted in Nickless, "The Origins of Shaker Feminism," p. 39.

55. Artemus Ward, *Vanity Fair,* Feb. 23, 1861; as quoted in Morse, *The Shakers and the World's People,* pp. 202-3.

56. Dickens relates: "We walked into a grim room, where several grim hats were hanging on grim pegs, and the time was grimly told by a grim clock, which uttered every tick with a kind of struggle, as if it broke the grim silence reluctantly, and under protest. Ranged against the wall were six or eight high stiff-backed chairs, and they partook so strongly of the general grimness, that one would much rather have sat on the floor than incurred the smallest obligation to any of them." A "grim old Shaker" informed Dickens that the Society "had advertised but a few days before, that in consequence of certain unseemly interruptions which their worship had received from strangers, their chapel was closed to the public for the space of one year." Charles Dickens, *American Notes for General Circulation,* vol. II (London: Chapman and Hall, 1842), pp. 214-15.

57. Ibid., pp. 215-16.

58. Ibid., p. 217. Dickens appears particularly outraged, because he returns to this theme, saying later, "There is no union of the sexes; and every Shaker, male and female, is devoted to a life of celibacy. Rumour has been busy upon this theme, but here again I must refer to the lady of the store, and say, that if many of the sister Shakers resemble her, I treat all such slander as bearing on its face the strongest marks of wild improbability." Ibid., p. 218.

59. This was her observation, even though her husband, Bronson, thought he noticed an uncommon harmony between the sexes. See, Amos Bronson Alcott, *The Journals of Bronson Alcott: Selected and Edited by Odell Shephard* (Boston: Little, Brown and Co., 1938), p. 154. Her entry is dated Aug. 26, 1843.

60. See Karen K. and Pamela J. Nickless, "Trustees, Deacons and Deaconesses: The Temporal Role of the Shaker Sisters 1820–1890," in *Communal Societies,* vol. 7. (1987): 16-24.

61. For a full treatment of this theme, see Sally L. Kitch, *Chaste Liberation* (Champaign: University of Illinois Press, 1989).

62. Youngs, *Testimony of Christ's Second Appearing,* 1856 ed., p. 533. See also part II, chapter 3.

63. C. E. Sears, *Duality of the Deity: or God as Father and Mother* (Rochester, N.Y.: Daily Democrat Steam Printing House, 1867), p. 3.

64. White, *The Motherhood of God* (1904 pamphlet edition), p. 2.

65. Perhaps not just Western culture, however. See Sherry Ortner, "Is Female to Male as Nature is to Culture?" in *Woman, Culture & Society,* Michelle Zimbalist Rosaldo and Louise Lamphere, eds. (Stanford, Calif.: Stanford University Press, 1974), as well as several other relevant essays in this collection.

66. Sally L. Kitch, *Chaste Liberation: Celibacy and Female Cultural Status* (Champaign: University of Illinois Press, 1989), contends that the Shakers, in spite of their admitted failings, held a feminist ideal due to their celibacy. Louis

J. Kern, however, gets the opposite impression from Shaker celibacy. *An Ordered Love: Sex Roles and Sexuality in Victorian Utopias—the Shakers, the Mormons, and the Oneida Community* (Chapel Hill: University of North Carolina Press, 1981).

67. See, e.g., Jean Humez, ed. *Gifts of the Power: The Writings of Rebecca Jackson, Black Visionary, Shaker Eldress* (Amherst: University of Massachusetts Press, 1981). It is difficult to determine how many racial or ethnic minority members there were in any given community, since the Shakers did not differentiate in their membership rolls. But from the 1830 U.S. Census figures we learn that at Watervliet, e.g., there were two blacks and twenty unspecified aliens out of 246 members; as quoted in Dorothy M. Filley, *Recapturing Wisdom's Valley: The Watervliet Shaker Heritage, 1775–1975* (Colonie, N.Y.: Albany Institute of History and Art, 1975), p. 49.

68. See, e.g., Ann Douglas, *The Feminization of American Culture* (New York: Avon, 1977).

69. Elder Frederick Evans entertained many such visitors in the second half of the nineteenth century, sharing his radical views with them. Tolstoy was interested in the Shakers and corresponded with them. See Morse, *The Shakers and the World's People*, pp. 231-36. American Transcendentalists were also interested. See, e.g., Priscilla J. Brewer, "Emerson, Lane, and the Shakers: A Case of Converging Ideologies," *The New England Quarterly*, 55 (June 1982): 254-275. For other possible communitarian connections with the Shakers see Kit Firth Cress, "Communitarian Connections: Josiah Warren, Robert Smith, and Peter Kaufmann," *Communal Societies*, vol. 7 (1987): 67-81; and Otohiko Okugawa, "Intercommunal Relations among Nineteenth-Century Communal Societies in America," *Communal Societies*, vol. 3 (1983): 68-82.

70. Sears, *Duality of the Deity*, p. 7.

71. The Shakers, as other communitarian experiments, always maintained a tension between connection with the world and withdrawal from it. See, e.g., Yaacov Oved, "Communes & the Outside World: Seclusion & Involvement," *Communal Societies*, vol. 3 (1983): 83-92.

72. Catherine Allen, *The Questions of the Day* (pamphlet, 1888), p. 5.

73. Nicholas Briggs, *God,—Dual* (pamphlet, n.p., n.d., circa 1887), p. 4.

74. White, *Motherhood of God* (1904 pamphlet edition), p. 8.

75. Nickless, "The Origins of Shaker Feminism," pp. 62-66, cites a few articles from the 1870s and 1880s that argue against strict sphere demarcations for males and females. Even so, the distinctive roles of the masculine and feminine aspects of God are not challenged in any of the literature I have examined.

76. Antoinette Doolittle, "God's Spiritual House, or the Perfected Latter Day Temple," in *The Shaker* (March 1871): 20-21.

77. Catherine Allen, *The Questions of the Day* (pamphlet, 1888?), p. 4.

78. White, *Motherhood of God* (1904 pamphlet edition), p. 5.

79. Brewer carefully documents reasons for the Shaker decline in *Shaker Communities, Shaker Lives*. See also, Brewer, " 'Numbers are Not the Thing for Us to Glory In': Demographic Perspectives on the Decline of the Shakers," *Communal Societies*, vol. 7 (1987): 25-35; and William Sims Bainbridge, "The Decline of the Shakers: Evidence from the United States Census," in *Communal Societies* (1984):19-34.

3. The Gender-Inclusive God in Shaker Theology

1. Only one other important Shaker theological work was published during this period: John Dunlavy's *The Manifesto*, 1818. It does briefly mention the gender-inclusive God doctrine (p. 515), but also makes a general reference to the importance of Youngs' work. Other published works during this period were not theological treatises per se, such as the Society's first hymnbook, *Millennial Praises* (see Procter-Smith for a delineation of the gender imagery there), and *Testimonies* (1816 and 1827 editions) of the earliest believers, mentioned in the previous chapter.

2. The four editions of Youngs, *The Testimony of Christ's Second Appearing:* 1st ed. (Lebanon, Ohio: John MacClean, 1808); 2nd ed. (Albany, N.Y.: Printed by E. and E. Hosford, 1810); 3rd ed. (Union Village, Ohio: B. Fisher and A. Burnett, Printers, 1823); 4th ed. (Albany, N.Y.: The United Society, 1856). Green and Wells, *Summary View of the Millennial Church* (Albany: Packard and Benthuysen, 1823).

3. See F. W. Evans, *A Short Treatise on the Second Appearing of Christ in and Through the Order of the Female* (Boston: Bazin and Chandler, 1853), and especially *Shakers Compendium* (New York: Burt Franklin, 1859, reprinted 1972); also William Leonard, *A Discourse on the Order and Propriety of Divine Inspiration and Revelation . . .* (Harvard: United Society, 1853); C. E. Sears, *Shakers, Duality of the Deity: or God as Father and Mother* (Rochester, N.Y.: Daily Democrat, 1867); A. G. Hollister, *Divine Motherhood* (pamphlet, n.p., n.d., circa 1887); Nicholas Briggs, *God,—Dual* (pamphlet, n.p., n.d., circa 1890); Antoinette Doolittle, *Thoughts Concerning Deity* (pamphlet, n.p., n.d.); White, *The Motherhood of God;* and Aurelia Mace, *The Aletheia: Spirit of Truth* (New York: AMS Press, second ed. 1907, reprinted 1974).

4. Paulina Bates, *The Divine Book of Holy and Eternal Wisdom, Revealing the Word of God; Out of Whose Mouth Goeth a Sharp Sword* (Canterbury, N.H.: The United Society, 1849).

5. Garrett explains that the earliest Shakers permitted only two books, the Bible and a spelling book, since they were on "a crusade to emancipate the faithful from what the world called education," *Spirit Possession and Popular Religion: From the Camisards to the Shakers* (Baltimore: Johns Hopkins, 1987), p. 198-99.

6. Joseph Meacham, *A Concise Statement of the Principles of the Only True Church According to the Gospel of the Present Appearance of Christ Together with a Letter from James Whittaker to His Natural Relations in England. Dated October 8th, 1785* (Bennington, Vt.: Haswell and Russell, 1790). Meacham doesn't even mention Ann Lee, but Brewer contends this was deliberate since he wanted to reach a wider audience. Brewer, *Shaker Communities, Shaker Lives* (Hanover/London: University of New England, 1986), p. 25. The second published work is Richard McNemar's *The Kentucky Revival; or, a Short History of the Late Extraordinary Outpouring of the Spirit of God in the Western States of America* (Cincinnati: John W. Browne, 1807). This is a historical work and does not discuss the Shaker doctrine of God.

7. J. P. MacLean lists the contributors as Richard McNemar and Matthew Houston, saying they are both linguists and biblical scholars. *A Bibliography of Shaker Literature with An Introductory Study of the Writings and Publications*

Pertaining to Ohio Believers (Columbus, Ohio: Fred. J. Heer, 1905), p. 7. McNemar had been a renowned Presbyterian minister before joining the Shakers during their initial western campaign. Although John Meacham and David Darrow signed the work, Andrews doubts whether they actually collaborated in it, but says that Youngs may have consulted McNemar, Worley, and Houston. In addition, Seth Youngs Wells edited the 1810 edition, McNemar worked with Youngs on the 1823, and Calvin Green revised the work with Youngs before its 1856 version; Andrews, *People Called Shakers*, p. 318, n. 140.

8. Mary Dyer, who wrote against the Shakers, contends "In this work there is a display of learning and erudition. The author appears to have been instructed in Latin and Greek languages; but the men whose names are subscribed to the work as authors, is well known, are not men of education, which are David Darrow, John Meacham, Benjamin S. Youngs. In this work the tenets of that blunt and illiterate woman, Ann Lee, expressed in a rude, confused and ambiguous manner, are digested, dressed up, and presented under a different form (by some persons more masterly than Darrow, Meacham, and Youngs) so they assume the aspect of a regular system." *A Portraiture of Shakerism, Exhibiting a general view of their character and conduct, from the first appearance of ANN LEE IN NEW-ENGLAND, DOWN TO THE PRESENT TIME. And certified by many respectible authorities.* (Printed for the author, 1822), pp. 115-16. Another apostate, William J. Haskett, contends the work largely reflects Meacham's sentiments. *Shakerism Unmasked* (Pittsfield: Walkley, 1828), p. 126.

9. Mary Dyer says "those writings are more recommended than those of the Prophets and Apostles." *A Portraiture of Shakerism*, p. 116.

10. William Haskett, *Shakerism Unmasked* (Pittsfield: Walkley, 1828), pp. 268-69.

11. Very few scholars have compared these four editions. Michael Taylor notes "there is very little change in the type of moral argument which it makes." The basic framework, he says, was both "stable and dominant" and able to "handle unchanged both the crisis generated by a new generation of leaders and . . . the rise of the new charismatics during the period of Mother Ann's Work." "An Ethical Analysis of Confessions, Celibacy, and Community of Interest in the Shakers from 1770 to 1905" (Ph.D. dissertation, Harvard, 1973). While I agree with this as far as it goes, I nevertheless note a subtle theological elevation of both Mother Ann Lee and the gender-inclusive God concept.

12. For example, in 1859 Frederick Evans says, "It seems scarcely possible to resist this evidence of a *dual order*, so 'clearly seen' throughout all the domains of nature . . . without proving that *God also is DUAL*, Father and Mother," Evans, *Shakers Compendium*, p. 107. Some forty years later, Briggs reiterates: "Throughout creation we find manifest the dual principle,—in the mineral, vegetable and animal kingdoms." *God,—Dual*, p. 2.

13. Marini finds this theological element in line with the rationalistic impulse of the age. "New England Folk Religions 1770–1815" (Ph.D. dissertation, Harvard, 1975), p. 400. For possible connections to the treatment of nature in the wider culture, see Conrad Cherry, *Nature and the Religious Imagination: Edwards to Bushnell* (Philadelphia: Fortress, 1980).

14. Youngs, *Testimony*, 1808 ed., p. 437.

15. Ibid.

16. Ibid., pp. 527-28.

17. Ibid., 1856 ed., p. 533.

18. Ibid., 1808 ed., p. 438.

19. Ibid., 1856 ed., p. 533. Although he quotes no Scripture passages here, he may be alluding to I Corinthians 1:24 and seeing this as providing information about the Godhead.

20. Youngs, *Testimony*, 1808, 1810, 1823 eds., (n.p.)

21. See, e.g., Elizabeth A. Johnson, "The Incomprehensibility of God and the Image of God Male and Female," in *Theological Studies*, 45:3 (Sept. 1984).

22. Youngs, *Testimony*, 1808 ed., p. 527.

23. Ibid., 1810 ed., p. 541; 1823 edition, p. 501. The stress is now on the two descents of the Spirit of God.

24. Ibid., 1856 ed., p. 533.

25. Ibid., 1808 ed., pp. 527-28. By the 1823 edition, Holy Spirit is changed to Mother, but with the same intent, p. 542.

26. Ibid., 1856 ed., p. 409; see 1808 ed., p. 462, which is slightly different. Note the Pauline influence.

27. Marini discusses the relationship of Shaker theology to Calvinism in "New England Folk Religions." See also Alan Heimart, *Religion and the American Mind from the Great Awakening to the Revolution* (Cambridge, Mass.: Harvard University Press, 1966); and Amanda Porterfield, *Feminine Spirituality in America: From Sarah Edwards to Martha Graham* (Philadelphia: Temple University Press, 1980) for an interesting analysis of the gender and God issue in the past two centuries.

28. Youngs, *Testimony*, 1808 ed., p. 449-50; 1810 ed., p. 454; 1856 ed., p. 396.

29. Ibid., 1856 ed., p. 526, see also pp. 528-32.

30. Ibid. See book 8, chaps. 3, 5, 6.

31. Ibid., 1810 ed., p. 438; 1856 ed., p. 383.

32. Ibid., 1808 ed., p. 44; 1810 ed., pp. 12-13; 1856 ed., p. 11.

33. Ibid., 1856 ed., p. 507.

34. Ibid., p. 531.

35. Green and Wells, *A Summary View*.

36. Brewer, *Shaker Communities, Shaker Lives*, discusses this in detail. See especially chapter 6.

37. Marini, "New England Folk Religions," p. 444; and see his references to Calvin Green's *Biographic Memoir* (ms. Sabbathday Lake, 1851) on p. 73.

38. Brewer, *Shaker Communities, Shaker Lives*, pp. 31-32.

39. Green and Wells, *A Summary View*, p. 91.

40. Ibid., pp. 91-92. Drawing again on Genesis 1:27, they say that: "it is certainly most reasonable and consistent with infinite Wisdom, that the image and likeness of God should be most plainly manifested in man . . . it must appear evident that there exists in the Deity, the likeness of male and female." The source is in the unity of the "creative and good principle."

41. Ibid.

42. For research in this area, see the comprehensive bibliography in Ruth Hubbard, Mary Sue Henifin, and Barbara Fried, *Women Look at Biology Looking at Women: A Collection of Feminist Critiques* (Cambridge, Mass.: Schenkman, 1979). And for a succinct and careful treatment of the classical underpinnings

(Aristotelian, Augustinian, Thomistic) see Kari Elisabeth Børresen, *Subordination and Equivalence: The Nature and Role of Woman in Augustine and Thomas Aquinas* (Washington, D.C.: University Press of America, 1981), esp. pp. 41-43, 192-95.

43. Green and Wells, *A Summary View*, p. 92.

44. Briggs, *God,—Dual*, pp. 2-3.

45. Ibid. Youngs also objects that the trinitarian view "makes a plurality of Gods"; *Testimony*, 1808 ed., p. 437. Green and Wells express a similar phrase, saying that the two are not "two *Persons*, but two *Incomprehensibles*," Green and Wells, *A Summary View*, p. 92.

46. Karl Barth deals with this issue and the difficulties of the word person in the doctrine of the Trinity. See *Church Dogmatics*, "The Triunity of God" (Edinburgh: T. & T. Clark, 1975), I:I:9.

47. Green and Wells, *A Summary View*, p. 93.

48. Ibid., p. 116.

49. Ibid., p. 215.

50. Ibid., pp. 130-32.

51. Ibid., p. 216.

52. Ibid., p. 131.

53. Ibid., p. 214

54. Ibid., pp. 218-19.

55. Ibid., p. 219.

56. Ibid., p. 217.

57. Ibid., p. 216.

58. Calvin Green, "Biographic—Memoir—of the Life and Experience—of Calvin Green," New Lebanon, N.Y. (WRHS, Shaker collection), VI:8-28, pp. 335-57.

59. Philemon Stewart, *A Holy, Sacred, and Divine Roll and Book* (East Canterbury, N.H.: The United Society, 1843). Stewart's work was seen by the Society as of such importance that some five hundred copies were printed and sent to the heads of various nations, as well as brought and read to each Shaker community by Stewart himself.

60. John McKelvie Whitworth, *God's Blueprints: A Sociological Study of Three Utopian Sects* (London and Boston: Routledge & Kegan Paul, 1975), p. 52. Whitworth asserts that Stewart's "revelations primarily consisted of a comprehensive restatement of the theology and history of the group," as opposed to the less-noticed Bates book.

61. E.g., Procter-Smith notes one in Harvard, 1807, *Women in Shaker Community and Worship*, p. 181; Eric Rohmann notes one in 1827, "Words of Comfort, Gifts of Love: Spirit Manifestations Among the Shakers 1837–1845" (B.A., Antioch College, 1971); Desroche says there were three revivals, *The American Shakers*, pp. 101-7.

62. See especially Brewer, *Shaker Communities, Shaker Lives*, chaps. 7 and 8.

63. For descriptions of this period see Brewer, *Shaker Communities, Shaker Lives*, chap. 7; and Rohmann, "Words of Comfort, Gifts of Love."

64. Hervey Elkins, *Fifteen Years in the Senior Order of Shakers: A Narration of Facts, Concerning that Singular People* (Hanover: Dartmouth Press, 1853), p. 35.

65. Passive receptivity, inspired speech, and even trance-like states are typical of prophecies that spring from claimed spirit possession. See Garrett, *Spirit Possession and Popular Religion*. However, it needs to be considered

whether the stress is greater in justifications for spirit messages delivered by females than those by males.

66. Bates, *Divine Book of Holy and Eternal Wisdom*, pp. 692-95.

67. Ibid., p. 501 note.

68. Ibid., see, e.g., p. 661.

69. Ibid., p. 141. For a history of this common interpretation of *kephale* (head), see Linda Mercadante, *From Hierarchy to Equality: A Comparison of Past and Present Interpretations of I Cor. 11:2-16 in Relation to the Changing Status of Women in Society* (Vancouver, B.C.: G-M-H Books [Regent College], 1978).

70. Bates, *The Divine Book of Holy and Eternal Wisdom*, p. 249.

71. Ibid., p. 277.

72. Ibid., p. 298.

73. Ibid., pp. 502-3 note.

74. Ibid., p. 502.

75. Ibid., p. 505.

76. Ibid., p. 191.

77. Ibid., p. 240.

78. Ibid., pp. 510-11.

79. Ibid., p. 508; see also pp. 278 and 505.

80. Ibid., pp. 536-38.

81. Ibid., p. 509. See also Eve's testimony, pp. 615ff.

82. Ibid., p. 153.

83. Ibid., p. 317.

84. Ibid., pp. 96, 132.

85. Ibid., pp. 153-54.

86. Ibid., pp. 280, 449.

87. Ibid., p. 534.

88. Ibid., p. 661.

89. Ibid., p. 536.

90. Ibid., p. 205.

91. Ibid., p. 41.

92. Compare Ezekiel 3:1-3.

93. Bates, *The Divine Book of Holy and Eternal Wisdom*, p. 298.

94. Ibid., p. 275.

95. Ibid., note, p. 275.

96. Ibid., p. 297.

97. Ibid., p. 543.

98. Antoinette Doolittle, "God's Spiritual House, or the Perfected Latter Day Temple," in *The Shaker* (March 1871): 20-21. But even though she was a very prominent Shaker writer, Doolittle did not consider herself a theologian, lamenting, "I wish I were a thorough historian, a theologian and something of a logician." "Were Moses and Jesus Free-Agents?" in *The Shaker* (Dec. 1871): 94-95. See also Anna White and Leila Taylor, *Shakerism: Its Meaning and Message* (Columbus, Ohio: Fred J. Heer, 1904).

99. The way Bates practiced and achieved recognition of her ministry is one hallowed by time, and in some respects it parallels the way certain female mystics performed priestly and prophetic functions in medieval Catholicism. A similar dynamic through which authority was recognized is well described by Caroline Walker Bynum in *Jesus as Mother: Studies in the Spirituality of the High Middle Ages* (Berkeley: University of California Press, 1982).

4. The Visitations of Holy Mother Wisdom and God the Father and the Testimonies of Shakers

1. F. W. Evans, *Autobiography of a Shaker, and Revelation of the Apocalypse* (Mt. Lebanon, n.p., 1869), pp. 36-37. The fact that he lists wisdom as a masculine attribute is unusual since generally Power was the masculine side and Wisdom the feminine.

2. *Report of the Examination of the Shakers of Canterbury and Enfield Before the New-Hampshire Legislature, at the November Session*, 1848, p. 27.

3. See Edward R. Horgan, *The Shaker Holy Land: A Community Portrait* (Harvard, Mass.: The Harvard Common Press, 1982), pp. 78-86.

4. F. W. Evans, *Autobiography of a Shaker*, 2nd ed. (New York: American News Co., 1888), pp. 40-41.

5. Edward Deming Andrews, *People Called Shakers* (New York: Dover, 1963), pp. 154, 159-60.

6. Hervey Elkins, *Fifteen Years in the Senior Order* (Hanover: Dartmouth Press, 1853), p. 56.

7. "A Record of Holy Mother Wisdom's First Visitation on the Holy Mount. Copied for the Ministry. New Lebanon. June 1, 1842" (WRHS, Shaker collection), VIII:B159, p. 196; and "True Record of the Visit of Holy Mother Wisdom" (WRHS Shaker Collection), VIII:B10. Another account is described by J. P. MacLean, *Shakers of Ohio: Fugitive Papers Concerning the Shakers of Ohio, With Unpublished Manuscripts* (Columbus, Ohio: F. J. Heer, 1907), pp. 394-96. Since the Shakers were careful record-keepers, other full or fragmentary accounts of these visitations may exist in individual community and private collections. Yet it is also likely that more accounts were written than have been preserved since later in their history the Shakers expunged or neglected many of the records from this period.

8. See, e.g., David Lamson, *Two Years Experience Among the Shakers: Being a Description of the Manners and Customs of that People, the Nature and Policy of their Government, their Marvelous Intercourse with the Spiritual World, the Object and Uses of Confession, their Inquisition, in Short, a Condensed View of Shakerism As It Is* (West Boylston: David R. Lamson, 1848), pp. 93-97; Polly Vedder, "A Spiritual Journal or Record of many beautiful and precious Gifts and presents received from our Heavenly Parents in the world of Spirits . . . ," vol. II, n.p., May 23, 1841 (WRHS Shaker Collection); as quoted in Rohmann, "Words of Comfort, Gifts of Love," (B.A. Thesis, Antioch College, 1971) p. 20; as well as the testimonies discussed in this chapter.

9. "A Record of Holy Mother Wisdom's First Visitation," passim.

10. Ibid., p. 12.

11. Ibid., pp. 8-9.

12. Ibid., passim.

13. "True Record of the Visit of Holy Mother Wisdom " (WRHS, Shaker Collection), VIII:B10.

14. "A Record of Holy Mother's First Visitation" notes that the preparation for the second visitation began in late September and was preceded by one of Wisdom's angels who came in November to explain a message from the Godhead. Testimonies from Harvard, e.g., note at least three visits of Holy Mother Wisdom and one of God the Father. See section on testimonies.

15. Lamson, *Two Years Experience*, passim.

16. Ibid., p. 93.

17. Ibid., pp. 93-96.

18. Vedder, "A Spiritual Journal or Record," May 23, 1841, as quoted in Rohmann, "Words of Comfort, Gifts of Love," p. 20.

19. From the accounts it appears that Wisdom met with the entire community together at meeting. But Polly Vedder describes Wisdom first meeting with sisters and brothers in their dwelling rooms (thus they would be segregated by sex) and then jointly in meeting. Vedder, "A Spiritual Journal."

20. Lamson, *Two Years Experience*, p. 101.

21. See, especially, Procter-Smith's section, "Women in 'Mother Ann's Work'," where she discusses, among other things, the various gifts as using symbolism from women's work in particular, such as the "Sweeping Gift." *Women in Shaker Community and Worship*, pp. 196-203.

22. See Procter-Smith, *Women in Shaker Community and Worship*, pp. 191-96, for the range of contemporary interpretation about this period.

23. Lamson, *Two Years Experience*, p. 103.

24. Elkins, *Fifteen Years in the Senior Order*, pp. 55, 75.

25. Henry C. Blinn, in his important account of the period, *The Manifestation of Spiritualism Among the Shakers 1837–1847* (East Canterbury, N.H., n.p., 1899), pp. 36-38, only barely mentions the "ministration of Holy Mother Wisdom," focusing on the purification rituals but not on her actual visit. Other later writers as well were especially careful to play down those elements deemed unacceptable by subsequent generations.

26. Lamson, *Two Years Experience*, p. 95.

27. Elkins, *Fifteen Years in the Senior Order*, p. 34. Louis Kern elaborates on this point, *An Ordered Love: Sex Roles and Sexuality in Victorian Utopias—the Shakers, the Mormons and the Oneida Community* (Chapel Hill: University of North Carolina, 1981), pp. 106ff.

28. Seth Y. Wells, [untitled testimony], New Lebanon, N.Y.: May 15, 1843 (WRHS, Shaker Collection), VI:A6.

29. Lamson, *Two Years Experience*, p. 45.

30. Ephraim B. Prentis, [untitled testimony], Watervliet, N.Y., Dec. 23, 1943 (WRHS, Shaker Collection), VI:A11.

31. Elkins, *Fifteen Years in the Senior Order*, p. 35. See also, e.g., the Testimony of Ephraim Prentis, who describes instruments' efforts to resist the spiritual manifestations, to no avail. "I have seen those who strove to withstand this power, so violently exercised, that if not for that power which possessed them, they must to all appearances be dashed in peaces [sic], and thus would continue to be wrought upon until they was [sic] willing to perform what was required of them."

32. It is possible that this call by the elders was made in response to the 1843 publication in Philadelphia (and thus the eastern Shakers would be most affected) of an anonymous book describing the spiritualist exercises being practiced by the Shakers in this period, *A Return of Departed Spirits of the Highest Characters of Distinction, as well as the Indiscriminate of All Nations, into the Bodies of the "Shakers," or "United Society of Believers in the Second Advent of the Messiah." By an Associate of Said Society* (Philadelphia: J. R. Conlon, 1843).

33. Diane Sasson lists these dates, *The Shaker Spiritual Narrative* (Knoxville: University of Tennessee Press, 1983), p. 69. And the directive from the elders is also quite evident in the frequent inclusion in testimonies of, e.g., "according to request from my lead" and "in union with the present gift." Thus, "Written

by me, according to request from my lead whom I love and am willing to obey."
Cilenda Wardwell, [untitled testimony], Enfield, Ct., Dec. 15, 1843 (WRHS,
Shaker Collection), VI:A-2. "I feel called upon in union with the present gift to
give in my testimony and declare my faith in this gospel of Christ's Second
Appearing." Charles Sizer, [untitled testimony], New Lebanon, N.Y., Dec. 21,
1843 (WRHS, Shaker Collection), VI:A-6. "Not willing to miss of the blessing
which is gained by the cross, I will labor in obedience to the present gift, to
write something of my faith respecting the way of God." Carsandana Benton,
[untitled testimony] Enfield, Ct., Dec. 21, 1843 (WRHS, Shaker Collection),
VI:A-2.

34. "Record of the Church at Watervliet, N.Y." (WRHS, Shaker Collection),
V:B279.

35. Most (53 out of 60) of the testimonies used from the period of Mother
Ann's Work were written between March and December, 1843.

36. George Stroup says that in conversion there is a collision of perspectives
(building up and extending Hans Georg Gadamer's graphic hermeneutical
metaphor of fusion), *The Promise of Narrative Theology: Recovering the Gospel in
the Church* (Atlanta: John Knox Press, 1981), p. 209.

37. Stroup, *Promise of Narrative Theology,* pp. 173-75, 96-97.

38. The Shakers, although communitarian, nevertheless show marks of
individuality in their narratives. In this theirs are similar to Puritan conversion
narratives which contain, buried within an apparent standardization, a
self-conscious selection process which allowed the individual to shape "the
narrative which was finally allowed to stand as the image of his [sic] soul."
Daniel Shea, *Spiritual Autobiography in Early America* (Princeton: Princeton
University, 1968), p. ix. But the Shaker testimonies were closer in purpose to
the contemporary narratives from England, i.e., "a vehicle for evangelical
comfort and encouragement," like those which grew out of the English
" 'experience meetings' or 'conferences' in which the saints already admitted to
church communion edified one another with further accounts of their
experiences." Patricia Caldwell, *The Puritan Conversion Narrative: The
Beginnings of American Expression* (Cambridge/New York: Cambridge University, 1983) pp. 35, 76.

39. Sasson, *Shaker Spiritual Narrative,* p. 211. Shakers were also similar in this
to the Puritans who "sought to assemble the evidence for divine favoritism
toward him," often presenting this "to convince the elders that the presence of
grace was evident in their experience" in that it had "conformed, with
allowable variations, to a certain pattern of feeling and behavior," Shea,
Spiritual Autobiography in Early America, pp. ix, 91.

40. When Shaker narratives allude to the difficult journey, both physically
and spiritually, that led the writer to the Shaker way, it is similar to many
Quaker journals which "recount the protracted search of the narrator for
Truth, which he inevitably finds in the doctrines of the Society of Friends."
Shea, *Spiritual Autobiography in Early America,* ix.

41. Sasson, *Shaker Spiritual Narrative,* pp. 211, 18.

42. These are likely not all the testimonies that were produced during this
period, but the ones the Shakers thought worthy of preserving or copying.
They are most copiously available in the Western Reserve Library collection.
The other Shaker collections examined do not reveal large numbers of
additional testimonies.

43. Not all of the sixty testimonies were completely legible, and a number do

191

not give biographical data such as birth date or age at joining. Thus these figures have to remain approximate. The study was restricted to eastern communities, and these particular villages were chosen since they represented the most copious source of testimonies. Although a number of very interesting spiritual autobiographies also exist in this collection, for the sake of uniformity the study was restricted to items designated specifically as testimonial. These particular items, it is assumed, would have been specifically written at the ministry's request to testify to the manifestations of the revival.

44. At the first reading, this might not be competely clear, since the word Mother is frequently used for both Mother Ann and Holy Mother Wisdom. The revival testimonies follow the pattern of the earlier style of testimonies which solely referred to Ann Lee. These earlier testimonies were later redacted. Thus "terminologically . . . Ann Lee was differentiated from Holy Mother Wisdom, the Mother-analogue of the Godhead. 'Our blessed Mother' reflected the person of Ann Lee, the Shaker founder, the spiritual Mother; 'Holy Mother Wisdom' identified God as Mother in complement to God as Father." Thomas Swain, "The Evolving Expressions of the Religious and Theological Experiences of a Community: A Comparative Study of the Shaker Testimonies from Oral Traditions to Written Forms as Preserved in Four Documents," *Shaker Quarterly*, 12 (Summer 1972): 49.

45. Phebe Smith, [untitled testimony], Watervliet, N.Y., n.d. (WRHS, Shaker Collection), VI:A11.

46. David Buckingham, [untitled testimony] Watervliet, N.Y., Dec. 22, 1843 (WRHS, Shaker Collection), VI:A11.

47. Ephraim Prentis, [untitled testimony].

48. E.g., Matilda Wells, [untitled testimony], Watervliet, N.Y., Dec. 23, 1943 (WRHS, Shaker Collection), VI:A11.

49. One in January 1843, two in April, one in May, one in September, two in November, and the rest between December 10 and 23.

50. The Harvard believers may have been more sensitive to these worldly experiments; they and several of the other Shaker communities had significant contact with utopian, communitarian, and socialistic ventures. For connections that Harvard Shakers had with Fruitlands and Millerites see, e.g., Horgan, *The Shaker Holy Land*, pp. 78-86. For some discussion of the general contact betwen utopian ventures, see, e.g., Kit Firth Cress, "Communitarian Connections: Josiah Warren, Robert Smith, and Peter Kaufmann," in *Communal Societies* vol. 7 (1987): 67-81; and Otohiko Okugawa, "Intercommunal Relations among Nineteenth-Century Communal Societies in America," in *Communal Societies*, vol. 3 (1983): 68-82.

51. The testimony of Samuel Myrick, Harvard, Oct. 15, 1843, identifies one visit as occurring in the summer of 1841. The testimony of Lucy Myrick, Harvard, June 18, 1843, indicates that a visit took place in 1842. The testimony of Lucy Clark, Harvard, Aug. 20, 1843, mentions there have been three visitations of Wisdom. The testimony of Susan Channel, Feb. 29, 1844, mentions a visit from Wisdom in the spring of 1841 and describes, but does not date, a visit from the Father. And the testimony of Mary Ann Widdifield, Harvard, Mar. 30, 1845, notes that a visit from the Father took place in 1844. (WRHS, Shaker Collection), VI:A11. The Millerites generated much excitement during this same period, with the major prediction set for between March 1843 and March 1844, then revised to October 1844.

52. The Grosvenor family (which had converted together) was influential in the Harvard community at that time, especially Roxalana. She was instrumental in preserving and redacting the earlier type of Shaker testimony and demonstrated her spiritualist concerns by the way she edited these documents. Her influence may have been substantial. Several of the Grosvenors were later expelled or disgraced, however. See Horgan, *The Shaker Holy Land*, especially pp. 103-4. The large and important Myrick family also seemed especially attracted to feminine imagery for God (see below).

53. Two existing community studies (on Harvard and Watervliet) do not analyze the revival period in enough depth to answer this question, but they do give some helpful background. See Horgan, *The Shaker Holy Land;* and Dorothy M. Filley, *Recapturing Wisdom's Valley: The Watervliet Shaker Heritage, 1775-1975* (Albany: Town of Colonie and Albany Institute of History and Art, 1975).

54. Elijah Myrick, [untitled testimony] Harvard, Sept. 3, 1843 (WRHS, Shaker Collection), VI:A5.

55. Samuel Myrick, [untitled testimony].

56. Daniel Myrick, [untitled testimony], Harvard, Sept. 10, 1843 (WRHS, Shaker Collection), VI:A5.

57. Susan L. Channel, [untitled testimony].

58. See, e.g., Lucy A. Fairchild, [untitled testimony], Watervliet, N.Y., Dec. 23, 1843 (WRHS, Shaker Collection), VI:A11; and also Lucy Clark, [untitled testimony].

59. Susan L. Channel [untitled testimony].

60. Mary Ann Widdifield, [untitled testimony], Harvard, Mar. 30, 1845 (WRHS, Shaker Collection), VI:A5.

61. Ibid.

62. Susan L. Channel, [untitled testimony].

63. James Wilson, [untitled testimony], New Lebanon, N.Y., Dec. 19, 1843 (WRHS, Shaker Collection), VI:A6.

64. Daniel Sizer, [untitled testimony], New Lebanon, N.Y., Dec. 20, 1843 (WRHS, Shaker Collection), VI:A6.

65. Thomas Damon, [untitled testimony], Enfield, Ct., Dec. 23, 1843 (WRHS, Shaker Collection), VI:A2.

66. James Mott, [untitled testimony], New Lebanon, N.Y., Dec. 23, 1843 (WRHS, Shaker Collection), VI:A6. His testimony can be found with those of New Lebanon, and the dating is in the same period as theirs, but in another record he is listed as having joined at North Union, Ohio. Since Shakers were often transferred (or left and returned) from one community to another, it can at times be difficult to trace their residences.

67. David A. Buckingham says that "Mother Ann's visitation and cleansing work began in this place" in late 1838, and some were "chosen by our blessed Mother as instruments, thro' whom to convey her mind and will to her children."

68. Roba Blanchard, [untitled testimony], Enfield, Ct., Dec. 19, 1843 (WRHS, Shaker Collection), VI:A2.

69. Nancy Ann Blandin, [untitled testimony], Enfield, Ct., Dec. 22, 1843 (WRHS, Shaker Collection), VI:A2.

70. Orren Haskins, [untitled testimony], New Lebanon, N.Y., Jan. 7, 1842 (WRHS, Shaker Collection), VI:A6.

71. Mary Ann Widdifield, [untitled testimony]. See also, e.g., Chauncy Sears, [untitled testimony], New Lebanon, N.Y., Dec. 21, 1843; and George Wilcox, [untitled testimony], Enfield, Ct., Dec. 23, 1843 (WRHS, Shaker Collection), VI:A6; and Lucy Clark, [untitled testimony].

72. Orren Haskins, [untitled testimony].

73. Lucy Clark, [untitled testimony].

74. E.g., see the testimonies of the orphans' Mary Ann Widdifield, Julia Ann Avery, Enfield, Ct., Dec. 19, 1843 (WRHS, Shaker Collection), VI:A2; and Roba Blanchard. Angus Jennett also attests to having found "fathers and mothers in the gospel," Dec. 23, 1843 (WRHS, Shaker Collection), VI:A11. And see Testimony of Elijah Myrick.

75. Whitworth, *God's Blueprints*, p. 49.

76. Marini, "New England Folk Religions 1770–1815" (Ph.D. dissertation, Harvard, 1975), p. 484.

77. Clifford Geertz, "Religion as a Cultural System," in *Anthropological Approaches to the Study of Religion*, Michael Banton, ed. (New York: Frederick A. Praeger, 1966), pp. 1-46, see esp. p. 36.

5. The Shakers and Contemporary Theology

1. This was very similar to the ideal behavior for mothers in the Oneida community. See, e.g., Louis J. Kern, *An Ordered Love: Sex Roles and Sexuality in Victorian Utopia—The Shakers, the Mormons, and the Oneida Community* (Chapel Hill: University of North Carolina Press, 1981), p. 289-90; and for this and related issues, see Ellen Wayland-Smith, "The Status and Self-Perception of Women in the Oneida Community," *Communal Societies*, vol. 8 (1988): 18-53.

2. Caroline Walker Bynum makes a related point in discussing the use of female imagery in the Middle Ages. See *Jesus as Mother: Studies in the Spirituality of the High Middle Ages* (Berkeley: University of California Press, 1982).

3. Elizabeth A. Johnson has formulated this schema in "The Incomprehensibility of God and the Image of God Male and Female," *Theological Studies*, 45:3 (Sept. 1984).

4. Hans Küng, e.g., although he does not linger over the point, talks about the "feminine-maternal element" of a God still imaged primarily as masculine. *Does God Exist?* (Garden City, N.Y.: Doubleday, 1980), p. 673.

5. Johnson, "The Incomprehensibility of God and the Image of God Male and Female," p. 456.

6. For a brief overview of this option, see John Dart, "Balancing Out the Trinity: The Genders of the Godhead," *The Christian Century* (Feb. 16-23, 1983): 147-50.

7. See, e.g., Anne Fausto-Sterling, *Myths of Gender: Biological Theories About Women and Men* (New York: Basic Books, 1985); and Ruth Hubbard, Mary Sue Henifin, and Barbara Fried, *Women Look at Biology Looking at Women* (Cambridge, Mass.: Schenkman, 1979).

8. Richard of St. Victor, *The Twelve Patriarchs. The Mystical Ark. Book Three of The Trinity*, Classics of Western Spirituality (New York: Paulist, 1979). See book 3 of *The Trinity*, chapter 15, and also chapter 21 where Richard explains that "Shared love is properly said to exist when a third person is loved by two

persons harmoniously and in community, and the affection of the two persons is fused into one affection by the flame of love for the third," p. 392.

9. See, e.g., Joan Chamberlain Engelsman, *The Feminine Dimension of the Divine* (Philadelphia: Westminster, 1979), who also traces this theme through other traditions.

10. For a brief attempt at this see, e.g., Küng, who speaks of the "feminine-maternal element," *Does God Exist?*, p. 673. For an overview of scriptural bases for this tradition, see Leonard Swidler, *Biblical Affirmations of Woman* (Philadelphia: Westminster, 1979), pp. 21-73. Leonardo Boff speaks of the feminine dimension in Jesus, and feminine connotations for Spirit, but also says that "this is not just a matter of introducing feminine figuration into the Trinity . . . but of working out the feminine dimension of the whole mystery of the Trinity and of each of the divine Persons." He nevertheless distinguishes between masculine and feminine symbolism, *Trinity and Society* (Maryknoll, New York: Orbis, 1988), p. 122, also pp. 120-21, 182-83. But see also Boff's *The Maternal Face of God: The Feminine and Its Religious Expressions,* translated by Robert R. Barr and John W. Diercksmeier (San Francisco: Harper & Row, 1987); and Donald L. Gelpi *The Divine Mother: A Trinitarian Theology of the Holy Spirit* (Lanham, Md.: University Press of America, 1984).

11. Johnson, "The Incomprehensibility of God and the Image of God Male and Female," p. 458.

12. Jürgen Moltmann offers both a critique of strict monotheism as the source of the monarchical, patriarchal view of God, and some suggestions about gender-inclusivity in a reconceived trinitarian view of God. *The Trinity and the Kingdom: The Doctrine of God,* (San Francisco: Harper & Row, 1981), pp. 164-65 and passim.

13. Johnson, "The Incomprehensibility of God and the Image of God Male and Female," p. 460.

14. See, e.g., Phyllis Trible, *God and the Rhetoric of Sexuality* (Philadelphia: Fortress, 1978); idem. *Texts of Terror: Literary-Feminist Readings of Biblical Narratives* (Philadelphia: Fortress, 1984); and Virginia Ramey Mollenkott, *The Divine Feminine: The Biblical Imagery of God as Female* (New York: Crossroad, 1981).

INDEX

197

AQUINAS COLLEGE LIBRARY
35060001907206

WITHDR